The Making of Myth

EDITED BY

RICHARD M. OHMANN

G. P. PUTNAM'S SONS, NEW YORK, 1962

ACKNOWLEDGMENTS

Of the essays in this volume, those by Dorson, Kluckhohn, Eliade, Wolff, and Bruner originally appeared in *Daedalus,* the Journal of the American Academy of Arts and Sciences, under the editorship of Gerald Holton, and are reprinted with the permission of the Academy. These essays, along with the pieces by Murray and Frye, were assembled in *Myth and Mythmaking* (New York: George Braziller, 1960), and Braziller has also consented to this re-use of the materials. Joseph Campbell's "Transformations of the Hero" is from Part II, Chapter 3 of *The Hero with a Thousand Faces* (Bollingen Series XVII, New York, 1949), and appears here by permission of The Bollingen Foundation. Eliade's "The Yearning for Paradise in Primitive Tradition" originally appeared in *Diogenes,* Summer 1953, and The University of Chicago Press, publisher of *Diogenes,* has granted permission for this use of the essay.

FIRST PRINTING

Library of Congress Catalog Card Number: 62-12846

Printed in the United States of America. Published on the same day in the Dominion of Canada by Longmans Canada Limited, Toronto.

CONTENTS

A NOTE TO THE INSTRUCTOR

The essays in this book will, by themselves, provide students with much to think and write about. The several authors differ enough in assumptions and emphasis so that paper assignments may usefully require comparison of two or more essays, and in doing so lead students to serious thought about the nature of myth. Some topics of this kind are listed at the end of each essay. But *The Making of Myth* will serve best, I believe, if the student reads it in conjunction with one of the books (or part of one) listed in the bibliography. Of course it would be ludicrous to imply that the student, after exposure to this book, will be able to do a professional analysis of a myth. But he should learn enough about possible ways of dealing with myth to make confrontation with an actual myth or tale quite rewarding. After the bibliography are some suggested topics for papers to this end. Ideally, the student should first read *The Making of Myth* to an accompaniment of class discussion, should then write an explicative, speculative, or critical essay based on the materials in the book, and finally should attack a myth or collection of myths on his own. But this is in no sense an indispensable cycle: either type of paper can be assigned without the other, and no doubt still more approaches to the subject will suggest themselves.

THE MAKING OF MYTH

INTRODUCTION

RICHARD M. OHMANN

A myth is not literally true, not to the person who refers to it as a myth. So the word "myth" has taken on a pejorative use: we speak contemptuously of "the myth of Aryan superiority," or we dismiss flying saucers as "just a myth." Believers may be annoyed to hear Christianity called a myth, or a mythology, and one group of Bible scholars have bent their efforts for a hundred years to disentangle truth from myth in their field, in order to point to the historically verified residue, be it large or small, and say "Here is what a respectable believer can build his faith on." Our century likes true propositions—facts—and would prefer not to be deluded by fairy tales, so we think. To label something a myth is, for many, to place it in an inferior rank, well below science, news, and even fiction, which, after all, lays no claim to literal belief the way live myths do.

Then, too, we associate myths with primitive cultures especially, cultures that faded before our scientific revolution or that are too remote or benighted to have shared it. School children study the Greek or Norse or American Indian mythologies either for their own sake, as pretty stories, or as examples of the way in which men ignorant of the world's workings seek to explain what they see and feel. Civilization pushes myths aside, it would seem. By the fourth century B.C., Greece took a lighthearted attitude toward its gods. The Roman state retained the old mythology as its official reli-

1

gion, but statesmen went through the necessary rituals cyn-
ically, without belief. The American Indian, absorbed by
industrial society, gradually comes to think of his myths
simply as traditional stories. Fewer and fewer Christians hold
the story of Genesis to be literally true; many value the
ethical content of their religion without assenting to its account of *what happened*. An impatient scientific culture tends
to think of myths as vestiges of an earlier, groping stage in
human development, best forgotten.

And yet myth dies hard. Serious scholars continue to be
seriously concerned with it, as the present volume bears witness. More significantly still, literary artists continue to work
the mines of myth. Yeats reshapes Irish legends to his own
ends and builds a personal mythology from scraps of theos-
ophy and medieval lore. Dramatists like O'Neill, Anouilh
and Cocteau use the Greek plays as sources, not merely from
a conviction that the old stories are best, but out of an appre-
hension of permanent meaning in them. Among the novelists,
Joyce constructs his major work on the model of the Odyssey,
and weaves almost all the western myths into *Finnegans
Wake,* while Faulkner creates a myth of his own from the past
and present of Yoknapatawpha County. Of course a society
in which professors study myths historically and anthropolog-
ically and in which a few artists self-consciously adopt a
mythical frame of reference is a long way from a society in
which bards retell legends around a fire to credulous listeners.
Still, the fascination that myths currently hold for the literary
and scholarly imaginations evidences the durability of the
mythical in human experience.

Why does myth deserve such permanence? For one thing—
and this is the least that can be said—the study of myth is interesting because it promises insight into a phase of development that all cultures pass through. The creation of myths is
seemingly a universal activity of primitive and not-so-primi-
tive man, and one that has crucial importance for him. We
better understand his needs, his relationship with nature, his
aspirations, by understanding the myths he lives by. But this
is only the beginning. Primitive people, after all, are people.
They confront the mysteries of birth, pleasure, suffering, and
death, as do we. They too are fathers and mothers, wives and

husbands, sons and sisters (though their domestic arrange-
ments are not always like ours), and in these roles they are
proud, puzzled, loving, and resentful, as are we. They hunger,
thirst, and desire. They must deal with an external world
which, different as it is from New York or Our Town, presents analogous beauties and dangers, and seems alternately
generous and refractory in answering to their wants, just as
our world does. The shape of life is, in many of its important
contours, much the same for them as for us, and it is with life
as grasped by the human mind that myths concern themselves.
Myths comment on the world, and in a deeper way they comment on man. To understand myths and the needs they serve
is to understand something about ourselves.

And not only by analogy, at that. I have been writing as if
man had altogether stopped looking at life from a vantage
point of myth, but surely this is an exaggeration. Aside from
the special appearances of myth in literature and other works
of our high culture, there are countless signs that the mythical
imagination survives, even in Western civilization. The Bible
is far from a mere historical text for many Christians and
Jews, and, however remote their God is from the anthropomorphic Old Testament deity, men still invoke him in their
affairs: how many times a week do the newspapers speak of
our struggle against godless communism? In more homely
ways, too, we have our myths and partial myths. Several generations of Americans, for whom Horatio Alger's heroes represented universal types, grew up to a myth of worldly success,
mysteriously granted to the virtuous and denied the un-
worthy. For decades the Western, with its endless rearrange-
ments of a few plots and its portentous comment on good and
evil, violence and gentleness, manliness, brutality and cow-
ardice, has held the interest of young and old Americans. A
good deal of myth surrounds our national heroes, from Washington to Davy Crockett. New accretions of myth constantly
gather around temporary heroes like James Dean and Jack
Kerouac. And, most telling of all, the individual psyche goes
on restlessly creating symbols and mythically transforming
conscious life in dreams. As Joseph Campbell has it, "In the
absence of an effective general mythology, each of us has his
private, unrecognized, rudimentary, yet secretly potent pan-

theon of dream." * Is myth still with us? More than we are perhaps inclined to think.

At any rate the impulse to myth remains within us, and more than one serious intellectual (including some represented in this book) looks back nostalgically rather than condescendingly to periods of broadly accepted myth, and half wishes for a new mythology to shape our world view. For myth can be regarded as a healthy, life-giving activity of the human mind, rather than a primitive aberration of rationality. In myth and dream there is an outlet for the most profound psychic drives, those which our surface life commonly ignores, or suppresses, and which, if not confronted, can rise up to plague the conscious mind in a thousand ways. Too, myths have an exemplary function. They give concrete embodiment to man's ideals, his vision of a better self and a better world.

The essays in this volume are thus an introduction to a subject of continuing importance. The approaches vary. Henry A. Murray's first piece is an extended effort to define myths by their content, their meaning, their use, the circumstances under which they arise, and the needs that produce them. The other essays have narrower scope. Richard M. Dorson examines critically some methods of interpretation which scholars have brought to bear on myth. Clyde Kluckhohn, taking a broad anthropological view of the subject, catalogues some mythical themes that appear in a wide range of cultures. Northrop Frye outlines the role of myth and mythic thought in poetry. Then follow three treatments of actual myths, or rather mythic clusters. Mircea Eliade examines traditions of Paradise in primitive mythology and in Christianity, drawing a connection between the yearning for Paradise and the experience of mysticism. Joseph Campbell dissects the universal myth of the hero. Robert Lee Wolff follows a mythlike ideology through its development and subsequent influence on actual historical events, a reminder that myths have consequences. With Jerome S. Bruner's essay we have a somewhat different approach. Although he discusses myths of "the happy man," his principal aim is to consider what happens when myths, with their capacity for externalizing inner ex-

* *The Hero with a Thousand Faces* (New York, 1949), p. 4.

perience and dramatizing human ideals, become inappropri-
ate to the needs of individuals and communities. The present
is such a time, Bruner contends, and Murray agrees; in a brief
postscript the latter suggests that traditional myths are obsolete, and wonders what sort of replacement we now need. The
essays add up to a self-contained treatment of the subject, and
the bibliography lists some collections of myths and folk tales
from various parts of the world, to which students may wish
to refer for detailed study.

DEFINITIONS OF MYTH

HENRY A. MURRAY

Most mythic narratives consist of fusions (*complex* myths) or of sequences (*serial* myths), or of both fusions and sequences of *simple* (component) myths. Each of these simple myths can stand alone and constitute a separate tale, or be incorporated as a part in an otherwise non-mythic narrative. The myth of miraculous birth, for instance, is a component of various heroical, *serial* myths, but it is nonetheless often recited and celebrated by itself in its own right, as it is with us on Christmas day. Anyhow, from now on I shall generally be using—for brevity's sake—the singular form, "myth," "story," or "event," rather than repeating in each instance, "myth or compound of myths," "story or series of stories," "event or chain of events."

The following definitions are arranged according to as-

HENRY A. MURRAY, born in New York City in 1893, received an M.D. degree from Columbia University in 1919, and later a Ph.D. in biochemistry from Cambridge University, England. After four years at the Rockefeller Institute for Medical Research, he was trained in psychoanalysis and succeeded Dr. Morton Prince as director of the Harvard Psychological Clinic. After service with the O.S.S. in World War II, he joined the new Department of Social Relations at Harvard, and became professor of clinical psychology in 1950. He was co-author of *Explorations in Personality* (1938) and of *Assessment of Men* (1948). He is an expert on Herman Melville, whose *Pierre* he has edited.

pects, under each of which one or more kinds, or classes, of myths may be distinguished.

1. *Formal, descriptive definition. A myth manifestly consists of the essential features of an important, more or less natural/preternatural situation or event (that has a basic thema) in which at least one extraordinary, more or less natural/preternatural psychic entity is involved—all this as sensibly represented in one channel or another.* Let us consider this definition part by part.

1.1. *an event (series of actions or interactions) sensibly represented in one channel or another,* that is, a myth is *not* an actual occurrence, but an occurrence (more or less actual/ imaginary) represented in sensory terms, *not* in conceptual, theoretical terms. To the early Greeks *mythos* meant "the thing spoken" or uttered by the mouth (Spence [1]), including "the thing spoken during a religious ceremony." Since these were magical words identical with their meanings, one could say that *mythos* referred to *both* the actual *words* which represented the preternatural (imagined) event enacted by the mute performers of the rite, *and* the preternatural (imagined) **event** represented by the words. The preternatural event consisted chiefly of the imagined actions of one or more gods, the audible imitation (description) of which by means of words and the visible imitation (enaction) of which by means of muscles was felt to be unquestionably efficacious. From these sacred tales and rituals, in imitation of the imagined actions of *superhuman* beings, evolved the written and then audibly spoken and visibly enacted secular tragedies of the Greek theater in imitation of the imagined actions of unusual *human* beings. The term that Aristotle gave to the events or series of actions represented by the masked actors of the drama was *mythos* (translated "plot").

Research indicates that many of the stories incorporated in the works of Homer and Hesiod were descended from ritual narratives. Though greatly altered in the course of transmission, these were still called "myths" and, in subsequent centuries, characters and episodes from these mythic tales were depicted time and time again in vase paintings and in sculpture. Thus, it is not contrary to Greek usage to say that a myth may be not only a story, or event represented in words, but also an event enacted in a ritual or drama, and that a part-myth may be one or more climactic moments of an event depicted in some durable medium. Besides these, there is another channel of representation which is central to them all, namely the imagination. This is so because an event must be covertly visualized (recollected, dreamed, or consciously fabricated in the mind) before (or during) its theatrical enaction, its narration, or its depiction in a bas-relief or drawing. Furthermore, an overtly represented event must be registered in the mind by its receptors (spectators, auditors, readers); and, then, if it is to endure in a state of readiness for numerous subsequent transmissions, it must be recurrently reproduced in the stream of consciousness. In short, to account for the creation and propagation of myths in variant versions, there must be composers, transmitters, receptors, conservers, and recomposers of mythic patterns. I am proposing, then, that we distinguish the following channels of representation:

(i) an imagined (visualized) representation of a mythic event: a *mythic imagent* (imagined event). This approaches the definition of myth as a "large controlling image." (Schorer)

(ii) a verbal (visualizable) representation of a mythic event in speech or writing: a *mythic narrative.*

(iii) a quasi-actional (visible and audible) representation of a mythic event: an *enacted myth,* a *mythic drama or rite.*

(iv) a material (visible) representation of a mythic situation or of one or more mythic characters or moments of a mythic event: a *depicted myth* or *mythic icon.*

Here my first purpose is to substitute "event sensibly represented" for "story," because the latter, though usually more convenient, is ambiguous: it points (too exclusively) to spoken or written language as well as to the actions described by the language. My second purpose is to introduce *imagent* (an imagined—dreamed, fantasied, recollected, predicted, or fabricated—event), in preference to "image"—which points to a single, more or less stationary entity or configuration, a still-shot of a moment in the sequence of events—as a suitable word to designate the covert unit central to all mythic transactions. A book of mythic stories on a shelf in the library is inoperative—a mere residue of past imaginations—so long as it is never read, never generates influential imagents in other minds. "Imagent" is also consonant with the psychoanalytical conception of myth as a collective dream or fantasy.

What is common to all the above-listed channels of representation (some of which are nowadays commonly combined —in cinema, TV, comics, etc.) is their appeal to the emotions through the senses, chiefly through internal or external vision, but also through the ear, and even through the nostrils (e.g. incense in a religious ceremony). For this, "sensible" (sensuous) seems to be a suitable term, indicating that myth belongs in the domain of art in the broadest sense, that is, belongs with what is art to children, to primitives, to the multitude, to professional critics, or to the artist, whether or not it serves the aims of religion, morals, politics, or commerce. Its concrete, "sensible" (graphic, figurative, visualizable) representations distinguish it from the general, conceptually abstract, imageless, and emotionally uninvolving diction of science and philosophy, as well as of much ordinary thought and speech. The utility of the word "sensible" is that it is not (like "artistic" or "aesthetic") restricted to the sense-qualities enjoyed and valued by gifted and experienced appreciators, the sense-qualities say, of acknowledged works of art, of impressive religious ceremonies or monuments, of eloquent political rhetoric, and so forth. "Sensible" is equally applicable to tawdry, unartistic, visual representations (e.g., a cheap "chromo" of the Crucifixion), to low-grade, commercial art, such as advertising (cf. *The Mechanical Bride,* McLuhan [2]), and indeed, to all grades of graphic portrayals, from the lowest to the highest, encountered, for example, in today's mass media. Thus, according to this view, every myth is an event sensibly represented; but only a relatively few, sensible representations can be properly called "myths," and of these some are cherished as great art (e.g., certain poetical passages in *Isaiah*), whereas others lack aesthetic properties. Whether or not a mythic narrative or mythic icon (e.g., cave painting, picture of Madonna and Child) is *valued* as a work of art, depends, in each case, on the genius of the composer.

1.2. *a represented event in which at least one extraordinary psychic entity is involved,* that is, *every* actor in a mythic event is *not* an average, all-too-human mortal. Among the early Greeks "myth" came to mean a story "about the gods," that is, about supposedly supernatural, immortal beings. But not exclusively, because in a large number of their mythic stories the immortal gods, either by conjugating among themselves or by conjugating with mortal beings, begot human sons and daughters with whom they were thenceforth almost necessarily involved. Furthermore, these immortals of the Hellenic imagination, being often more quarrelsome than peaceful and very interested in mankind, were constantly meddling and taking sides in the disturbed affairs on earth—giving victory to some favored hero, impeding the endeavors of a person who angered them, rewarding the virutuous, humbling the vain, or elevating some abused heroine or hero to the high bowl of heaven to survive there in the form of an immortal constellation. Hence, a "story about the gods" was a story which had one or more genuine gods or goddesses in its cast, and *also,* in most cases, other less exalted characters, say, a demigod or demigoddess, a mortal hero or heroine, a prophetess, an old crone, a nondescript hermit, a few animals, or a monster of one fabulous variety or another. Later there were so-called "myths" in which the veritable gods were not at all involved (e.g., Narcissus, Daedalus, Icarus, and so forth) or no more than the God of Christianity would be involved in a modern story about the general of an army who devoutly prayed for victory. In due course, as mentioned earlier, *mythos* was applied by Aristotle to dramas about men and women of superior estate (e.g., Agamemnon and Clytemnestra), who were believed to be actual, historical persons. They became purely fictional to later "more sophisticated" generations; but now once again, since the excavations of Schliemann and his successors, they have been restored in many minds to the status of authentic human beings. Anyhow, do we not find inseparable gradations between venerated human beings (culture heroes, founders of religions, kings, emperors) and unmistakable gods? Alexander the Great was a god at the oasis of Ammon, Captain Cook a god in the Hawaiian Islands.

Although these considerations make it impossible to assert that all or most myths, in the Greek sense, are stories about the gods, it can be said that the vast majority of them are about one or more very *extraordinary* psychic entities. By "psychic (anthropopsychic rather than anthropomorphic) entity" I mean an animate creature or even an inanimate object that is described as perceiving, feeling, thinking, or intending as a human person does. This or some equivalent expression is required in order to embrace all the principal participants in primitive myths. An anthropopsychic entity may have a natural anatomy (animal or human), a preternatural anatomy (gigantic, weird, some combination of animal and human features), or no designated anatomy at all (a bodiless psyche, Holy Ghost, God). But whatever his or her embodiment or lack of embodiment, at least one psychic creature (hero or heroine) in a mythic story has cynosural, charismatic potency, that is, attracts and binds attention, interest, wonder, awe, dread. This attractive force is generated by the recognition that the being is in some or most respects *extraordinary*: omnipotent, omniscient, or uncommonly beautiful, powerful, grave, reckless, wise, virtuous, or evil—a creator, progenitor, provider, seductress, leader of a great migration, founder of a society, lawgiver, ruler, warrior, implacable enemy, priest-king, prophet, seer, magician, healer, savior, killer of killers, technical inventor or benefactor, victor in a decisive contest. Often the decisive factor is the degree to which receptors become identified with the hero of the story. It seems that mythmakers have since time immemorial been almost exclusively interested in natural or preternatural superior beings, say in the aspirations of a king or of an elite group. In some myths a highly valued sect or a whole collectivity is "hero."

1.3. *the essential features of an important event that has a basic thema,* that is, a represented *mythic event* is distinguished from all other events (represented in dreams, fantasies, folk tales, novels, dramas, ceremonies, pictures, and carvings) by its great "importance" to human beings, its relevance to their origin, survival, development, happiness, or glory. Furthermore, although the representation of a mythic event may contain any number of nonessential features, it must include its "essential features," that is, it must set forth concrete, sensible exemplifications of its complete *thema* (thematic pattern).

Later on I shall bring up the problem of *partial* representations of a complete event and representations of an *incomplete* event. A single mythic image in the mind, in a poem, or depicted in a painting (e.g., Axis Mundi, Tree of Knowledge, Angel, Virgin Mary) is, in my terminology, a *part* of a myth (*mythic object, mythic character, mythic symbol,* or *moment* of a myth), a part which is very commonly sufficient to bring the complete mythic event to the consciousness of those who are familiar with it. In other cases, we may be dealing with a myth in a process of formation and hence with the imagination of an as-yet-incomplete event.

For lack of suitable English words pertaining to processes in time (in contrast to material configurations in space) "event" is commonly used to designate a single process completed in a fraction of a second (micro event) as well as to designate a manifold of proceedings with a far greater temporal span (macro event, e.g. the Thirty Years' War). For present purposes, however, an event may be defined as an arbitrarily selected *chronological series of interdependent activities* (succession of interacting endeavors) which has a *unitary character,* marked by a definable beginning, middle, and ending, the nature of which (beginning, middle, and ending) differentiates this temporal unit (time segment) from preceding and succeeding happenings, and in terms of which (beginning, middle, and ending) this unit may be sufficiently formulated. According to this view, an event may be of any *span* (duration) and of any spatial *scope* (size and distance of the terrains of action), and of any social *compass* (number of characters involved), provided it can be suitably designated by a single formula *(thema),* simple or complex. For example, the simple formula, oProhibition→sTransgression→oPunishment, might abstract the essential features of a myth with a span of a few minutes, or one, such as the famous Garden of Eden interaction, in which the passage of time between the beginning and the middle or between the middle and the ending terms was apparently much longer.

Since a *simple* thema is apt to be a very general statement, not sufficiently specific and distinctive for most purposes, one usually requires a more or less *complex* thema. For instance, the above-given formula for the Garden of Eden story might be supplemented with terms indicating that the prohibitor was God, that the prohibition was not to eat of the fruit of the Tree of Knowledge, that a tempter (serpent) was involved, that there were two transgressors, male and female (both "extraordinary" in being the first human creatures on this earth and progenitors of our species), that the transgression was prompted by curiosity, and finally that the form of punishment was expulsion from an idyllic environment, with no promised possibility of forgiveness and readmission. So much for a single temporal unit and its simple or complex formulation.

Most mythic narratives and dramas, however, are composed of two or more *different* temporal units, and hence cannot be epitomized by a single formula, simple or complex. These may be called *serial* myths, consisting, as they do, of a progression of causally related single myths, a progression which can be formulated only by a chain of simple or complex themas. The myth of the hero is a typical *serial* myth. Eventually we may have to go further, and distinguish myths which have a single, superordinate (overall, major) thema and a number of minor, component themas, sub-themas, and sub-sub-themas, some of which may be irrelevant to the major thema. More of this later.

This usage of "myth" and "thema" seems to conform to Aristotle's "myth" and "plot-structure," because for him "myth" was synonymous with "plot" and "plot" meant the sequence of concrete dramatic transactions, or, in other words, "the chain of incidents which are gradually unfolded in the story of a play" (Webster). A "plot" in this sense could be set forth by giving a reasonably full account of the enacted events, divorced from other aspects of the drama, such as the spectacle, diction, thought, and so forth. But "plot," for some critics, means "the plan or scheme of a literary creation" (Oxford English Dictionary), not the theatrical execution of the plan. In this sense, "plot" corresponds to Aristotle's "structure of the plot," an abstract, let us say, of the essential components of the enacted course of events, with special emphasis perhaps on the climactic enaction. Thus my *serial thema* (series of thematic patterns) is equivalent to Aristotle's "structure of a plot," or "structure of a myth," except that "thema" (a somewhat more technical word) is presented in terms which are usually more abstract than Aristotle's and always more abstract than the conventional "synopsis" of a dramatic story. This distinction between (a) "plot" as the chain of events visibly and audibly enacted and (b) "plot" as an abstract model of this chain is considered crucial, because the former is something "given" in the drama, something about which almost all receptors can agree, whereas the latter is the "construct" of a formulating critic; and . . . differences between constructs of this nature may be fundamental enough to generate protracted arguments among scholars. A myth, then, is an imagined event characterized by a certain thema (the best statement of which may be a matter of debate), but *not* the thema *per se;* because a thema is a *brief, conceptual* (imageless and undramatic) formula, which by itself lacks the myth's power to evoke emotions.

A *mythic event* is "important" partly because it involves an extraordinary, interest-binding psychic entity (e.g., Whale), but mostly because it is or has been *critical* and *consequential* to the welfare of a sociey as a whole or of most of the individual members of a special cult or great religion. Because the presence or absence of this characteristic is usually obvious to a reader of a written myth, it is included in this *formal,* descriptive definition; but the acid test is whether the represented event was or is felt to be important by its composers, receptors, conservers, and transmitters (part of a *functional* definition).

Generally speaking, a represented situation and endeavor is felt to be important if there is much at stake: if it is a question of nonexistence (nothingness) or existence (creation), chaos or order, extinction or survival, being killed or killing, decay or renewal, death or resurrection; a question of gaining, preserving, or losing some highly valued region, position, thing, person, or internal state of grace; a question of glory or humiliation, of the right to supreme authority, of ruling or being ruled, submission or defiance, being accepted or rejected; a question of prolonged captivity, liberation or escape; a question of moral good or evil, of transgression, punishment or pardon, of forgiveness or revenge, salvation or damnation; or a question of stagnation, death-in-life, or evolution, of challenge, catastrophe or creative coping.

A *mythic event,* as indicated earlier, is distinguished from all other, variously represented (non-mythic) events by the fact that it exemplifies a *basic* thema, clearly and dramatically, the themas involved in other classes of events being not only less fundamental or universal (basic), but less striking (harder to apperceive), because the engaged dispositions of the actors are mixed and weaker, adulterated by irrelevant elements, shaped by a particular culture in time, tempered by civilized restraints, and hence less primitive and deeply moving. Some day there may be some agreement as to the most acceptable criteria of "basic"; but in the meantime I shall define a "basic" thema as one which involves to a marked degree and in a dramatic form, emotions, wants, and actions, which are present as potential tendencies in virtually all men and women of all societies and times, a pattern of conflicting endeavors emanating from dispositions such as these: the craving for peace, security, serenity, or ecstasy; the force of lust, love, jealousy, or hate, of rage or fear, of hunger or avarice, suspicion or curiosity, of worldly ambition or lofty aspiration, envy, vanity, or pride, of exultation or creative zest, of loyalty, adoration, or compassion, grief or joy. Some of such strongly expressed dispositions will be embodied in the hero and some in other participants in the procession of events.

Before proceeding to other definitions of myth it might be clarifying to describe a little more explicitly than I have so far one possible way—a somewhat more detailed version of Aristotle's way—of analyzing a myth (plot, event) and formulating its thema (structure of plot). A reasonably complete statement of a thema should include:

(i) *Beginning: an abstract statement of the initial situation.* This might involve the specification of such variables as the state of the physical, social, cultural environment (e.g. the scene is laid in Hell, or the country is in a state of war, or a bitter religious controversy is in progress), or of such variables as the sex, age, relationships, position, traits, capacities, recent actions and present emotional state of each of the major characters (e.g., the life of a male child is threatened by a ruler who fears that the boy will eventually supersede him; or an intellectual recluse, satiated and enervated by years of orthodox scholarship, invokes the Devil; or a young prince is both outraged and depressed by the confirmed surmise that the new husband of his recently widowed mother is none other than his father's murderer.

(ii) *Middle*: *the thema proper*: *an abstract of the body of the represented event.* This consists of a brief specification of the mapor aim and endeavor of the hero, or, in more detail, if necessary, his successive proactions and reactions in relation to the environment, particularly in relation to one or more specific interacting entities, or characters (e.g., the vengeful hero searches for his injurer [a malevolent whale], encounters and attacks him; or the hero leads his people out of captivity and searches for land on which to settle).

(iii) *Ending*: *an abstract of the outcome, the terminal situation.* This defines the effects and consequences, or fate, of the hero's actions, the final state of affairs (e.g., the hero triumphs and marries the king's daughter; or the hero, overcome by guilt, puts out his own eyes; or the hero dies and is transported to heaven).

This is no more than a sketch of one among many modes of thematic analysis. Since, so far as I know, there is no widely preferred mode, decisions are bound to be largely arbitrary, a matter of taste or aim.

Although my own preferred method is to classify myths, whenever possible, in terms of the *thema proper* (middle term), most mythologists use a variety of methods, naming myths according to their most striking feature, at one or another level of abstraction (generality-specificity): initial mythic situation (e.g., idyllic environment, Eden), mythic hero or protagonist (e.g., androgynous deity, Herakles), mythic antagonist (e.g., werewolf, Satan), relationship of mythic characters (e.g., brothers, Cain and Abel), mythic *press*, or environmental force (e.g., flood, prohibition), mythic interaction (e.g., encounter with monster), terminal mythic situation (e.g., creation of the world, resurrection, paradise regained) and so forth. In Eliade's illuminating chapter one perceives the advantages, if not the necessity, of classifying at least some myths according to a certain kind of environmental situation or enjoyed inner state (e.g., Paradise), since this has been, on the one hand, a retrospected, preternatural *initial* situation from which humans were long ago expelled, and, on the other hand, a prospected preternatural *terminal* situation toward which their hopes have stretched: this progress into the future being equivalent to a regress into the past aiming at the ultimate restoration of the once-experienced, lost beatitude.

1.4. *a more or less natural/preternatural situation, event, or psychic entity involved,* that is, myths vary all the way from narratives almost all parts of which are preternatural (never been perceived, experienced, or known to occur—fantastic places, anatomies, capacities, and effects), such as the story of the creation of the world by a lizard, to narratives which are entirely natural (possible though not necessarily probable) except, say, for the intervention of a single preternatural being (god). And here the question is whether or not it is advisable to extend the traditional definition of a myth to include imaginations of important events with basic themas which are represented naturally, say, a realistic portrayal of the failure of a reckless astronaut to reach the moon—the myth of Icarus in modern dress. My proposal would be to call this a story with a *mythic thema* which was not mythically represented. In this connection we might note that a kind of achievement (e.g., flight) that would be preternatural (miraculous, impossible) in all preceding eras may suddenly become natural and commonplace.

The forces that are responsible for the course of mythic events are always psychic forces (agents, actors), never physical or chemical forces, and the representation is always concrete and sensible (not conceptual). The thema that a myth exemplifies, however, is abstract (a virtual universal), in the sense that it is a composite or generalization of countless human experiences or imaginations, divorced of all particulars.

2. *Referential definition.*

2.1. *Phenomenal reference. The manifest components of a myth—the represented situations, events, and actors—may mean what they literally appear to mean or may stand for anything else that is conceivable by man. It is here that we* run into the wars of the schools—many besides those men-

tioned by Dorson—in regard to the relative validity or significance of one or another mode of interpretation.

When we dream, everything we envisage is literally given,
the real thing; but as soon as we awake, it becomes either
meaningless, trivial, or symbolic of something else, and the
nature of this "something else" depends on our choice of
analyst. To the one who experiences it, a vision or hallucina-
tion may come as an animate actuality, the very presence, say,
of the creator and director of the universe; but to a psychia-
trist it may be nothing but an obvious wish fulfillment, the
projection of a bad conscience, or a powerful archetype
heralding an inflated psychic state. Who decides? There have
been times when a man's life might hang on whether he took
a sacred image or object literally or symbolically (e.g., the
forced confession of Berengarius that "the bread is not merely
a sacrament but the true body of Christ that is chewed with
the teeth"). A little later the orthodox way of taking it might
be the exact opposite. Evidently, what is literal truth to one
person, or to a person in a primitive state of mind, or to members of a particular cult, may be one or another variety of
symbolic truth to others, or sheer nonsense. To its composer,
a mythic composition may be consciously symbolic of one or
more things and unconsciously symbolic of several others,
none of which might correspond to the interpretations of its
inceptors. Think of the many proposed meanings of the
White Whale. To Starbuck Moby-Dick was "natural," because the traumatic mutilation of Captain Ahab's leg was
merely the involuntary reaction of a dumb brute. But to
Ahab the Whale was preternatural, the superhuman embodiment of a human psyche, or god, who acted deliberately out
of malice.

A mythic narrative, then, is usually susceptible of several
interpretations, some on different levels, each of which is
likely to contribute to our understanding of the full significance of the story. Of the major varieties of referents, it seems
that the largest consists of descriptions of the imagined
psychic causes of natural phenomena (although Freudian
psychoanalysts do not seem to believe that the imagination,
even of primitive peoples, is responsive to perils, harms, or
benefits coming from the physical or biological environment).

Leaving aside the question of which entities or kinds of entities were more influential in the composition of myths—the weather, sun, moon, Sirius, Orion, Milky Way, earth, mountain, volcano, sea, river, rain, fire, and so forth—*nature* myths can surely be distinguished as one great class, with *meteorological, astronomical, Terrestrial, chemical,* and *biological* (totem, monster) myths as sub-classes. All of these involve patent psychic projections (charming "pathetic fallacies") and hence nowadays can be entertained only on an emotional, poetical "as if" basis. They may contribute to our "feeling" for nature, but they add nothing to our understanding, and diminish, if anything, the effectiveness of our dealings with phenomena of these varieties. Perspections of a psyche in the earth have been replaced by knowledge of soil chemistry.

Besides animistic *nature* myths, there are those which refer to the states, actions, aspirations, and fortunes of a particular cult or whole society (*collective* myths); those which refer more particularly to the birth, experiences, endeavors, death, and afterdeath of an extraordinary human being or demigod —hero, king, savior (*individual* myths); those myths, social or individual, in which the prime actor is a transcendental preternatural being without embodiment in nature (*theistic* myths), and, finally, those which are chiefly concerned with internal, or endopsychic, occurrences or states (*intrapsychic individual* myths). Of course, these types are not mutually exclusive: a single, compound serial myth might include exemplifications of each variety. In fact, in primitive psyches, internal and external states are apt to change concurrently: the vigor of the earth, the vigor of the king, the vigor of the whole society decline together, the god of the past year, the old sun, is obviously dying; and when the young new god arrives, or the old one is rejuvenated, vigor and fertility are restored on all levels.

Analogous, in certain respects, to the visible cyclic transformations of the flora and fauna of the earth, of human bodies and of social groups, are the invisible but intimately experienced transformations of the psyche, self, or personality. It is to these that *intrapsychic* myths refer by means of imagery derived primarily from greatly modified percepts of external objects and events, much of which imagery had been projected into the environment. Thus myths of this sort involve a partial or complete withdrawal of projections, the projections of an earlier age, and a concentration on interior, intrapersonal developments: consequential subjective experiences, states of being or becoming, mutations of emotion and evaluation, interior conflicts and their resolutions. Poetic, mythic diction is not only the most natural and satisfying mode of expressing, representing and recording experiences of this sort, it is the only verbal means—particularly with the aid of ritual—of educing comparable emphatic experiences in other suitably receptive persons. Each mythic thema of this class is an abstract of countless personal experiences, set forth in concrete figurative language, all of which experiences, though necessarily both private and unique, are similar in certain significant respects, and thus common to a large number of self-conscious persons, generation after generation. In the last analysis, myths of this sort may be said to tend toward emotional and evaluational unanimity, toward shared subjective states and shared subjective knowledge through internal transformations. In contrast, science might be said to tend toward perceptual and conceptual unanimity, toward shared impartiality and shared objective knowledge through experimental manipulations of the environment. Mythic stories and symbols that depict the "night journey" of the introverted soul, the encounter with the monster in every person's "depths," liberation from imprisoning modes of feeling and of thought, reconciliation, spiritual rebirth, the beatific state of grace and redemption—experiences of this nature—are expressed in language that must be taken figuratively, symbolically, and imaginatively. Though the imagery is necessarily derived from the external world, the reference is internal. In no other way, as Plato insisted, can certain profound truths be genuinely conveyed to others.

This is a class of myths that were first generated and elaborated with the greatest subtlety in India. There, it seems, the solitary ascetic was inevitably more engaged in heroic encounters with his instincts—grown monstrous through perpetual frustration—than he was in dealing with the monsters of whatever environment he had deserted. This seclusive, inward, concentrated, private, and spiritual Hindu orientation

may be seen as the direct antithesis of the gregarious, outward, expansive, public, and material orientation of contemporary Soviet Russians as well as of Westerners generally,
especially North Americans. It is Jung more than anyone
perhaps who has worked with distinct success toward a synthesis of these opposites by applying Indian mythic images,
modes of thought, and wisdom in modified forms to the
dilemmas of Western man. One of his present theses, for example, is that our real enemies are within us—a horde of
frantically ambitious, vainglorious, and destructive dispositions—and our prime obligation is to cope with them at their
source rather than to project them into our ideological op-
ponents. Here intrapersonal (intranational) and interpersonal
(international) conflicts are mutually dependent, as they are
generally. But instead of holding that the international conflict must be settled before intrapersonal and intranational
serenity and good-will are possible, the order is reversed.

2.2. *Temporal reference. Myths are the essential features of
imagined situations or events (a) that occurred once upon a
time in the past, (b) that are destined to occur in the future,
or (c) that are now recurring, or have recurred and will continue to recur at regular intervals or in chronological order.*
All etiological myths (e.g., creation), unique environment or
event myths (e.g., paradise, catastrophe), social historical
myths (e.g., migration), and individual historical myths (e.g.,
life of a savior) belong to the first type (retrospective myths).
Interpretive myths descriptive of the forces responsible for recurrent seasonal changes (e.g., movements of celestial bodies,
fertility) or for a recurrent, chronological series of social or
personality changes (e.g., transformations of the self) belong
to the third type (*perennial* myths). Terminal, prophetic,
promissory, and apocalyptic myths (social or individual), descriptive of a unique mission, great encounter, and ultimate
better world (e.g., utopia, kingdom of heaven, world social-
ism, salvation, immortality, nirvana) belong to the second
type (*prospective* myths). All three types may be combined in
a complete metahistory of a society or metabiography of an
individual.

3. *Functional definition. A myth is an influential representation whose powers may be estimated in terms of the*

*social scope, the temporal span, and the average intensity of
its effects, these effects being of five classes: (a) cynosural-emo-
tional-memorable-inspirational, (b) convictional, (c) evaluational, (d) conational, and (e) integrational.* Let us examine
this definition part by part.

3.1. *cynosural, emotional, memorable, inspirational effects:*
a mythic representation is peculiarly and mysteriously attractive to the senses and imagination (vivid, impressive, enchant-
ing, spectacular, dramatic, marvelous). It becomes the focus
of rapt attention, excitement, wonder, thought, and talk
(cynosure), and leaves a durable and recurrent imprint in the
minds of its receptors (memorable). Its power in these respects
is often difficult to explain. Besides wonder, one or more
other emotions are generally involved: an affect corresponding to that of the hero or heroine of the drama (empathic
identification) or an affect, reciprocal or complementary, to
that of some represented entity (e.g., awe, fear, guilt in the
presence of an indignant deity). The representation may con-
sole, encourage, relieve anxiety, increase self-respect, or engen-
der hope, and, in addition, evoke and bind positive affection
(fellow feeling, love, gratitude, compassion, admiration,
adoration) for a major character in the story (e.g., Osiris,
Astarte, Adonis, Buddha, Job, Christ, Tristan, St. Joan, Don
Quixote, Hamlet, etc.).

Furthermore a myth inspires receptors with artistic gifts to
reproduce it in its original form or in variant forms and thus,
through chains of transmission, to propagate it down the generations. One measure of the value of a myth, then, is the
quality of the imaginative symbolism and of the works of art
which it inspires.

3.2. *convictional effects:* a mythic representation has a cognitive property, or function, in so far as it elicits belief or
faith in its essential validity or authenticity. Contrary to the
tenet of several of the foremost mythologists of the past century, this is not the primary function of most myths (it may
be the primary function of etiological myths); but it is a
necessary secondary or subsidiary function. A representation
of an event in which nobody has ever believed, literally or
symbolically, and/or in which nobody believes today, is not a
myth. Although it is generally agreed that a myth is a story

which "purports to be true," most people are quick to add
that a myth is, in fact, false, however true it may once have
seemed or may now seem to its adherents. For those who say
this, the stories or visions of the future in which they themselves believe and take to heart are not myths; only the stories
or visions cherished by those with whom they disagree are
myths. This major source of confusion and dissension calls
for a concerted effort to arrive at some acceptable solution.

First, let us note that the O.E.D.'s definition of "myth" as a
"wholly fictitious story" has no basis in antiquity, the term
having been initially employed to denote the exact opposite:
a sacred story, or an *hierophany,* as Eliade has called it—an
impressive, compelling manifestation of a spiritual force, an
epiphany of the superhuman psychic determinant of a critical
event. The fact that animistic nature myths and primitive
myths generally have been invalidated by science is not sufficient reason for asserting that *all* myths are false, by definition. Countless scientific theories have been similarly
invalidated, but this does not lead us to assert that *all* theories
are false. We say that theories are the best things science has
invented, even though the latest and best of these best things
are not considered to be wholly and precisely true.

It has already been pointed out that the linkage of "myth"
(the sacred truth of pagans) with "falsehood," as well as the
linkage of "gospel" with "truth," was hammered in by generations of Christian writers for reasons that are quite
obvious. But now that it is generally acknowledged that
Christianity itself has its ineradicable roots in myth, it is no
longer the religionists, but those whose conception of truth is
restricted to perceptible, objective facts who are most inclined to tie myth and falsehood in one package. This is to
be expected, since myth is a product of imperceptible (but no
less real and true) psychic states and dispositions and, in many
of its best forms, has reference to these; and, furthermore, a
large class of myths (*prospective* myths) refer to possibilities
in the as-yet-imperceptible future.

According to the definition here submitted, then, a live or
vital myth is a representation of a state, situation, or event
(past, current, or future) which, at its lowest, is accepted by its
carriers as sufficiently valid (credible, satisfying), or, at its

highest, is embraced as "the nearest approach to absolute truth that can be stated" (Coomaraswamy). Like a theory, however, a myth may not be credible to others, and it may cease to be credible, literally or symbolically, to those who formerly adhered to it; in which cases we might speak of an abandoned or *inert* myth. But it should be stressed that the convictional function of a myth is, in most cases, subsidiary to its conational function: it may be most effective when it provides no more than what is necessary in the way of an historical and contemporary perspective—say, a description of relevant antecedent events, of the current crisis, and of the desired outcome—to give meaning, significance, and urgency to some individual or social endeavor.

3.3. *evaluational effects:* one function of a myth is to propagate and periodically revive and re-establish veneration for the entities and processes it represents. Also, the myth itself, being highly valued, will ordinarily attain a superordinate, "sacred" position in the conscience of its carriers.

3.4. *conational effects:* these are of two kinds; the first is to excite and orient certain valued actional dispositions, guide conduct, and sustain effort (*educational* myth); the second is to do the opposite: to weaken or suppress certain disvalued actional dispositions (*deterrent* myth). By illustrating a basic aimful need, its actuation, and its outcome, undesirable or desirable, a myth presents a model, as does a parable, of what should be done if possible or of what should not be done under the given circumstances. It provides, one might say, a graphic exemplification of a precept, or even an operational definition of a possible scientific proposition: if in a *situation* of class 13, a man attempts an action of class 27, the *outcome* will be one of class 9. If the aim or action of an otherwise admirable hero is extravagant, vainglorious, shameful, or immoral and its outcome tragic, the story should produce, in susceptible receptors, an emphatic discharge and a subsequent reduction (weakening or suppression) of comparable, latent dispositions (*cathartic and deterrent* function). But if the aim and action of the hero or heroic group is admirable and the outcome happy (or even tragic), a potent myth will serve to encourage or sometimes imperatively impose comparable behavior. This I am calling the *educational* (drawing forth) function of a myth. We have such words as "imitation," "emulation," "actional identification" to describe what a witness of a conspicuous act may do; but, so far as I know, there is no common word—no word as suitable as "educe" ("education," "eductive")—to describe what the conspicuous actor (exemplar, eductor) is doing, intentionally or unintentionally. Eductional myths may be individual or collective.

Collective eductional myths of an especially potent species describe the alignment of forces already engaged or soon to become engaged in a crucial and decisive conflict, perennial or final. The forces which are in line with the group's welfare, with its hopes for the future, being beneficent in direction, are exalted as the good powers. The opposing and hence maleficent forces are portrayed as evil. It is a struggle-to-the-finish, then, between the forces of good and evil in one or another guise—light and darkness, renewal and decay, evolution and stagnation, unity and disunity, conservation and destruction, life and death—forces which have been commonly embodied in two opposing supernatural beings (e.g., God and Satan, Christ and anti-Christ, God and Allah), and more recently in two opposing -isms (e.g., Communism and Capitalism). According to this myth the triumph of the good force is inevitable, provided all become empathically identified with its objective and by certain prescribed co-actions assist in its achievement. Here the convictional function of the myth gives place to its conational function. The myth is conationally successful if it sets forth the confronting situation in such a way as to evoke social participation in acts which ultimately accomplish something.

3.5. *integrational effects:* a potent myth has the property of engendering unanimous passionate participation of all functions of the personality (*individual* myth), or of all members of a society (*collective* myth), and thereby of unifying and strengthening the person or the group. According to this criterion of the potency of a collective mythic ideology, the truth or falsehood of its representation of the group's present situation and future destiny, or the merit of the goal of the endeavor (as judged by posterity), or even the external effectiveness or ineffectiveness of the prescribed actions (ritual or actual) are of secondary importance: what counts is the achievement and maintenance of social solidarity (Durk-heim). A myth is valuable if it prevents disintegration, decadence, or civil war.

4. *Conditional definition. A ritual myth is an imagined event represented in words spoken by an appointed agent (e.g., shaman, priest, medicine man) during the event's cere-monial enaction at a prescribed place and time. Not all veritable myths are of this type.* Those who assert that "myth" means primitive *ritual* myth and nothing else are arbitrarily limiting the term to what is assumed to be the first public occasion and first purpose of a recited myth—say, to cooperate with the performers of a religious rite (enactors of the myth) in their efforts to imitate, assist, and influence a beneficent god or spirit in bringing about a desired state of society and of nature. I have called this type of semantic restriction the fallacy of phylogenetic primacy, because if we confine the ref-erent of a word (e.g., myth) to the first *known* appearance of a certain entity, this referent must be abandoned (e.g., ritual myths can no longer be called myths) if an earlier ap-pearance of the entity is subsequently discovered. Further-more, if we do this, every later appearance of the entity (e.g., the same sacred story recited under other conditions or with different aims, or various successive modifications of the story) must be designated by another name. My procedure has been to use adjectives to distinguish different kinds of myth.

I can see no good reason for excluding from the category "myth" all stories, no matter how primitive or sacred, whose association with a rite is neither traceable nor probable (e.g., numerous myths collected by anthropologists); exclude all stories which, during their descent from primitive, sacred (and maybe ritual) narratives, lost much of their primitive-ness and compelling sacredness as a result of the refinements and elaborations of story-tellers, poets, and dramatists—stories which were still about the gods (sacred in this sense) but which were no longer evocative of belief and veneration (not sacred in this sense)—e.g., the classical myths of Greece and Rome; exclude all less primitive stories about a person, such as Buddha, or the Virgin Mary, who made no claims to supernatural parentage and powers (not sacred in this sense), and yet is worshiped by millions as a supreme being (sacred in this sense); exclude all sublimated and symbolically re-interpreted descendants of early myths, which, though still held sacred and, in some cases, associated with a religious ceremony, have been purged of much of their original primitiveness (e.g., myths of Christianity, the Eucharist); and also exclude all cherished and widespread secular stories with mythic roots and characteristics that were composed within the last two thousand years in response to some state of affairs which, in certain respects, was unexampled in primitive societies (e.g., Faust myth in relation to Christianity, the Communist "apocalyptic" myth, Nazi myths).

As to the question of the priority of ritual and the invariable linkage of myth and ritual, it appears that those who cleave to this view are basing their judgments on documents drawn almost exclusively from the Near East (especially those descriptive of the death and rebirth rite); and though the theory is supported by many of the findings of recent, world-wide surveys, the amount of disconfirming data is at present so substantial that the rite-myth hypothesis can no longer be accepted as applicable around the globe. In the most comprehensive examination and judicious weighing of the evidence from primitive cultures that I have read, Kluckhohn [3] cites several instances of the composition of myths antecedent to the inauguration of a correlative ceremony, and of myths that are not associated and apparently have never been associated with ritual performances.

"To a considerable extent," Kluckhohn concludes, "the whole question of the primacy of ceremonial or mythology is as meaningless as all questions of 'the hen or the egg' form." A statement with which I heartily concur, because, as I see it, a mythic imagent (imaginal event: dream, fantasy, vision, trance, apperception, recollection), mythic narrative (event described in words), and mythic rite (event enacted physically), are interdependent, and all three related in some way to a given environmental situation or event. A mythic imagent—being either an imaginative apperception (interpretation) of an environmental situation or event, or this *plus* a vision of modifying the event in progress, of coping with the situation, improving or transforming it, or of escaping to a better situation—a mythic imagent constitutes the central variable in all transactions of this class, the patterned process intermediate between the evironment and any overt endeavor to respond to it effectively. Undisputed is the insight—generative of the profound rite-myth theory—that an act (say an instinctive act—analogous to a ritual—which is empathic with a movement in nature) precedes, in the chronology of a child's development, any—analogous to a recited myth—verbal description of the act. But here we are discussing elaborate *collective* rituals performed by adults, which evolved, we may suppose, from the simple to the complex down the generations; and it seems hardly possible that throughout this long history of ritualistic enactions, there were no dreams, fantasies, or visions (mythic imagents) about the gods to whom these ceremonies were addressed and no exchanges of these visions (mythic narratives) among those who were periodically participating in the elaboration of the rites. These considerations lead to a theory of interdependence, with any temporal order of the three overt channels of representation—narration, enaction, and depiction (e.g., cave paintings, figurines of Earth Goddess)—being possible, though not equally probable, and with the covert channel of representation—imagination—being almost inevitably prior to the other three.

5. *Causal definition. A myth is a product of imaginations oriented and sustained by one or more basic needs and feelings (dynamic psychic determinants) in response to a critical situation (instigational determinant) which is experienced, consciously or unconsciously, by the society as a whole, by members of a certain class, or by numerous individuals as persons.* I have already given illustrations of these and other classes of determinants, and a brief summary should be sufficient at this point.

The sense of empathic (mystical) participations with surrounding nature, projections of psychic beings, states and processes into environmental phenomena (e.g., Jehovah's voice in the hurricane), and the incongruous, preternatural figures and effects—exhibited in primitive myths, in the fantasies of children, the dreams of adults, the visions of highly creative people (e.g., Blake, Melville, Nietzsche), and the hallucinations of psychotics—may be partly attributed to the nature of the mental processes—the autonomous, disjunctive,

undirected and uncorrected sequences of imagents—that occur in primitive, fluid, intraceptive, dreamlike states of mind
(general *structural psychic determinant*). In other words, the
psyche of a mythmaker, ancient or modern, must be open *at
times* to influxions from the "depths" of the "unconscious"
("id" system). By primitives, such influxions were taken literally (as in a dream), but by modern poets they are eagerly
received and judged as possible symbolic or metaphorical
expressions.

To explain primitive man's awe of nature—fear of the dark,
biting animals, hurricanes, floods, and so forth—as well as his
daylight feelings of participation and reciprocation, another
factor should be added, namely, direct, unsheltered exposure
to the caprices of environmental forces (general *positional,
situational determinant*). But I have already said a good deal
—too much perhaps—about nature myths, and since man has
now gained considerable knowledge and control of physical
and chemical forces, and succeeded in contructing artificial
environments in which to live, nature has become less inti-
mate and less threatening to the majority of people and only
in our more poetic moods is it endowed with psychic attri-
butes. Henceforth, then, I shall confine myself to myths whose
referents are societies, special groups, two persons, a single
person, or components of a person.

I have already presented examples of critical situations
(instigational determinants) as well as of the fundamental
needs and emotions *(dynamic psychic determinants)* which
down the centuries have recurrently been involved in human
responses to these situations. The simplest formula is Freud's
(expanded to some extent): distressful stimulation leading to
a dream or fantasy of an object or person (e.g., breast, mother,
father, god, savior), of an external situation (e.g., idyllic environment, better world), of an external event (e.g., death of
enemy or rival), or of an act (e.g., murder, copulation, glorious
achievement) that will reduce the distressful stimulation (e.g.,
appease the aroused need). If the imagined, wish-fulfilling act
is consciously or unconsciously felt to be sinful or criminal
(e.g., parricide, incest), provoking to others or extremely
dangerous (e.g., flight), the dream is likely to include the
dreaded resultant of the act—retaliation, punishment, fall—

and thus serve as a deterrent. But now the person (dreamer) will be involved in another type of stressful state, namely, that of internal conflict between a strong primitive drive and an inhibiting fear of the consequences of its actuation. The kind of response that is now called for is one which will resolve the painful conflict, abolish anxiety, and restore the harmony of the personality as well as the harmony of whatever interpersonal relationships were involved.

Religions, myths, philosophies, and systems of psychotherapy have been largely or partly devoted to the achievement of unifying resolutions of this type and of more complicated types, in the society as a whole and/or in its individual members; and to the degree that any one of these systems succeeds in doing this—in preventing or relieving intolerable conflicts, curing "sick souls"—people will trust it, cling to it, believe in it, and conform to its prescriptions. Furthermore, to the extent that such high evaluations are shared by the population at large, the system will serve as a cohesive force. Thus, the relief of suffering, the gratification of the wish for spiritual unity and health, might well be added to the above-given *functional* definition of a myth. Here we happen to be viewing this achievement as one of the determinants of the myth's power to generate conviction and orient behavior. But clearly the two factors are mutually dependent: if a person is cured of an ailment he is more likely to be convinced of the truth of the correlative myth, and if he believes the myth he is more likely to be cured. As Julius Caesar is supposed to have said, "Most people believe what they want to believe."

What can be said about the origination or genesis of a myth? We are apt to talk—thinking of archetypes and the perennial philosophy—as if universal myths had been residing in man's mind since time immemorial. A better conception would be that of *mythic genes*—elements of mythic compositions—as very stable, potential image-tendencies, and yet perpetually engaged from generation to generation in a procession of compositions, decompositions, and novel re-compositions, so that it would be virtually impossible to point to a single mind as the place in space-time where a new, unexampled combination of mythic genes occurred for the first time.

A somewhat comparable difficulty is encountered in tracing the genealogy and allocating the credit for a new scientific proposition, such as the theory of evolution. But still we do point, with justice, to particular individuals as the ones who presided, each in his own way, over a revolutionary synthesis of ideas that occurred, unconsciously and consciously, in his head. Locating the origin of new mythic compositions is another matter: impossible in the case of prehistoric myths and not easy when it comes to modern myths. Myths are more likely to be formed unconsciously by slow degrees in many contemporary minds and must wait for their acceptance and propagation until the psyches of others are prepared for their reception. Also, recent myths are harder to identify: they are either veiled by the conceptual, discursive language of social ideology and social science (e.g., Marxism, Freudianism), or they are fragmentary, being still in process of cultural evolution.

In summary it may be said that the creative imaginations which participate in the formation of a *vital* myth must be those of people—often alienated and withdrawn people—who have *experienced,* in their "depths" and on their own pulses, one or more of the unsolved critical situations with which humanity at large or members of their own society are confronted. In other words, suffering in "representative men" may be one of the necessary determinants of an adequate response to challenge.

6. *Summary of definitions.* Disregarding nature myths (whose referents, in today's scientific terms, are physical, chemical, biological, and physiological entities and events), the following slight reconstruction of what has been said in this section may prove useful:

6.1. *mythic representation:* a sensible (sensuous, graphic), symbolic representation of an imagined situation or series of events, especially, today, a story or drama in poetic prose—not an abstract, conceptual (scientific) model of a certain class of events, nor an accurate, factual report of a specific event.

6.2. *mythic content:* a story which is manifestly about one or more extraordinary persons or preternatural psychic beings (e.g. god, whale, Frankenstein) or about a group or society as a unit, earnestly and wholly engaged in a series of important, critical endeavors (matters of physical, social, or spiritual vitality or death)—not about trivial people involved in inconsequential interactions.

6.3. *mythic thema:* a story which clearly, dramatically, and memorably exemplifies a basic or crucial (archetypal, virtually universal, or emergent and creative) plot structure—not a confused medley of several artificial, minor plots.

6.4. *mythic referent:* a story whose symbolism refers to intrapersonal, interpersonal, intrasocial, intersocial, or human-environmental states, forces, establishments, and interactions (conflicts), or to supernatural beings (e.g., extra-natural deities).

6.5. *mythic function*

6.51. *evaluational and conational function:* (a) *educational function:* a story which offers better values to its receptors, and—by presenting an example of a better type of action in a given type of situation, or of the solution of a distressful conflict, or of a better way of life or better target of endeavor —educes emulative efforts and thereby changes personalities and/or their modes of living. This is the chief criterion of a *vital* myth as contrasted with an *inert* myth; (b) *deterrent function:* a story which produces a catharsis and subsequent inhibition of an actional disposition.

6.52. *convictional function:* a story which is literally or symbolically credible to its receptors, congruent with reality, a story which portrays a form of interaction or a state of being which is realizable or conceivable, an outcome that is not impossible. Like a fable, it may be "a lie which tells the truth," or, like a parable, it may convey a particle of the wisdom of the ages or new wisdom.

6.53. *cynosural, emotional, or memorable function:* a story or drama in poetry or prose which "rejoices the aesthetic imagination" and leaves an indelible and recurrent impression.

6.54. *integrational function:* a large collection of sensible representations of events (mythology) which serves to unify a whole society.

Many modern works of literature satisfy a number of these criteria: 6.1, *mythic (symbolic) representation;* 6.4, *mythic referent;* 6.53, *mythic cynosural and emotive function;* and even 6.52, *mythic convictional function*—astonishing "the intellect with a new aspect of the truth." Of these, some are veritable exemplifications of 6.3, *a mythic thema* in modern dress. As for 6.2, *mythic content,* it seems that most artists and writers of our time are consciously oriented in the opposite direction, intent on describing trivial, impotent, neurotic, decerebrate, or hollow non-heroes, engaged in an essentially inconsequential sequence of events, who go out "not with a bang but a whimper." It is true that many highly intelligent young men—"Beats" in the broadest sense—have been empathically drawn in this general direction, but not with much zest and hope; and it would be hard to name a modern work which genuinely fulfills 6.51, *mythic evaluational and conational function* (either educational or deterrent). Of course we are a long way from 6.54, *mythic integrational function* (either individual or social).

This brings me to a question which, for certain obscure reasons, was postponed until this point: How shall we classify the numberless stories which exhibit some characteristics of a myth, however defined, as well as some characteristics of a nonmyth? Is there the slightest possibility of agreeing on a rule which will tell us what proportion of what characteristics (say, of the above-listed criteria) must be identified for a story to be called a myth rather than a nonmyth? Would it not be better, at least in debatable instances, to discriminate the mythic and the nonmythic parts or aspects of a story, instead of trying to decide into which of the two categories the whole medley should be forced? Personally, I would say "yes for the time being," and, instead of "myth," speak of "mythic contents," or "mythic thema," or "mythic function," and so forth.

Quite different from composing myths in mythic diction for mythic functions is the craftsman's use of one or more inert myths of antiquity as scaffolding for image sequences,

or in order to supply the learned with opportunities to identify recondite allusions, or to imbue his work with some
flavor of profundity—to do this, tongue in cheek, without
conviction or commitment.

No plenitude of mythic images, references, symbols, names,
or parallels can constitute a living myth, and, if used in this
sense, however sanctimoniously, "myth" will deteriorate into
a five-cent term and a counterfeit at that.

7. *Covert myths.* Very likely I have given the impression
that I am looking forward to the time when poets and artists
will collaborate in creating a saving mythology for mankind.
This is partly true, since out of admiration—and ignorance
no doubt—I am bent to the belief that the world cannot be
changed in a desirable direction and remain changed for
successive generations without the free and spontaneous collaboration of every form of art. Witness Christian art. But I
surmise—anyhow for our time—that creative ideas and creative lives will more generally precede it, though not by a long
span. What will inevitably come first are *covert* myths—
mythic imagents (visions)—which may be translated into theoretical language (the dominant diction of our time) and simultaneously or somewhat later into action, after which the
arts will come, and make the heretofore covert myths visible
to all.

Pertinent at this point is Whitehead's famous comment that
Christianity "has always been a religion seeking a metaphysic,
in contrast to Buddhism which is a metaphysic generating
a religion." [4] If we substitute "mythology" for "religion,"
and "metapsychology" or "metasociology" for "metaphysic,"
a discernible, ongoing cultural trend can be formulated in
this way: (i) a developmental metapsychology, (ii) partly
corresponding patterns of child-rearing, self-development,
and interpersonal relations, and (iii) partly corresponding
mythic themes represented in poetry, prose, and works of
art. In other words, these trends indicate an almost syn-
chronous and interdependent middle course between Buddhism and Christianity, closer to the former than the latter
sequence. An obvious example is psychoanalysis with its
novel, theoretical reconstruction of the Hebraic-Christian
mythology (e.g., the inherited trace of the original sin of

parricide from the prehistoric past, the imaginal recurrence in each child of the Oedipus drama, the upper superego in place of Heaven and Jehovah, the lower id in place of Hell and Satan, etc.). Also to be noted is the mutual influence of psychoanalysis and literature, and of psychoanalysis and personalities in process, the former shaped by observations of the latter and the latter shaped by the theories and practices of the former.

On the societal level we can observe in Marxism comparable, interdependent evolutions in the three spheres of activity: (i) an historical metasociology, (ii) corresponding patterns of social action, and (iii) a partly corresponding literature, all initiated and sustained by a secular form of the apocalyptic myth.

Communism, a mystique which tends toward war, tries to make the healthy into more effective social agents; and hence will have no truck with Freudianism, which is primarily concerned with the experiences of individual children, and with the disturbances of childhood as determinants of mental illness in adults as individuals. In process, possibly, is a mythology for peace and concord on the societal level, and, on the personal level, a mythology for successive stages of optimal development from adolescence to old age, as indicated by Erikson [5] for example.

8. *Part-myths.* Whoever is interested in modern myths will necessarily be alert to myths in the making, and hence to mythic fragments—covert images veiled by theoretical statements, symbols, metaphorical expressions, new enthusiasms, trends of thematic content in mass media, "explosions" of new slang, and so forth. The task is to extract mythic images and imagents from a large number of heterogeneous partial exemplifications and, if possible, to make a coherent whole of them.

NOTES

[1] Lewis Spence, *The Outlines of Mythology* (London: Watts & Co., 1944), p. 1.

[2] Herbert M. McLuhan, *The Mechanical Bride* (New York: Vanguard Press, Inc., 1951).

[3] Clyde Kluckhohn, "Myths and Rituals: a General Theory," *The Harvard Theological Review*, Vol. XXXV, No. 1, January, 1942.

4 Alfred North Whitehead, *Religion in the Making* (New York: Macmillan Co., 1926), p. 50.

5 Erik H. Erikson, *Childhood and Society* (New York: W. W. Norton & Co., 1950).

SUGGESTIONS FOR DISCUSSION

1. According to Murray, what would be necessary for an actual event or series of events—say the climbing of Mount Everest—to be transformed into a myth?

2. Murray stipulates that myths involve "at least one extraordinary psychic entity." Is this requirement sufficient in itself to exclude from the category of myth contemporary novels such as Fitzgerald's *The Great Gatsby*, Faulkner's *The Bear*, or Camus' *The Stranger?* Does it seem unlikely that our age will welcome tales of semi-supernatural beings, in Murray's sense?

3. Are the events of common fairy tales (e.g., those of the brothers Grimm) "important" enough to qualify as mythical? How do they engage (or fail to engage) the emotions in the appropriate way?

4. What is the difference between an event and a *thema?*

5. What are some possible referents of the story of Adam and Eve?

6. What characteristics of a myth make us reluctant to interpret it literally, make us look for a covert meaning? Answer the question with reference to one or more specific texts, such as the story of the Three Bears, Yeats' poem "The Second Coming," the *Aeneid*, the film "High Noon."

7. In what sense are myths "true" (see Murray's classification, section 3.2)?

8. To what extent does modern Christianity depend on convictional effects, and to what extent on emotional, evaluational, conational, or integrational effects?

9. How can a myth be said to satisfy the needs it arises from? Consider the Crockett myth, Little Red Riding Hood, the story of Romulus and Remus, *Oedipus Rex*.

10. Murray claims that most contemporary writers avoid mythic content and the mythic evaluational and conational function. Do you agree? What exceptions come to mind? If you agree, what conditions of modern culture do you see that might explain the phenomenon?

THEORIES OF MYTH AND
THE FOLKLORIST

RICHARD M. DORSON

Students of myth and folklore once occupied some common ground. In his often reprinted collection of essays called *Custom and Myth,* first published in 1884, Andrew Lang spelled out the relationship as seen by the anthropological school of English folklorists who so spiritedly advanced the cause of folklore science in the late nineteenth century. Two bodies of material intrigued Lang and his fellows. Around them they beheld archaic survivals among the British—and European—lower classes, in the form of village festival, agricultural rite, and household charm, so anomalous in the midst of the progressive, industrial, scientific England

---

RICHARD M. DORSON was born in New York City in 1916, and attended Harvard University as an undergraduate and graduate student, taking his Ph.D. in the history of American civilization in 1943. He has been professor of history and folklore, and chairman of the Committee on Folklore, at Indiana University since 1957. In 1956-57 he was Fulbright Visiting Professor in American Studies at the University of Tokyo. He is currently editor of the *Journal of American Folklore.* He has held Harvard Sheldon, Library of Congress, Guggenheim, and American Council of Learned Societies fellowships for library and field studies in folklore. His books on folklore include *Jonathan Draws the Long Bow; Bloodstoppers and Bearwalkers; Negro Folktales in Michigan;* and *American Folklore.*

of the Victorian age. From missionaries, travelers, colonial officers, and the new anthropological fieldworkers they learned about "savage" myths, usages, and beliefs in remote corners of the world. The equation between peasants and savages provided "The Method of Folklore," the title of Lang's opening chapter. Savage myth embodied in fresh and vivid form the withered superstitions and desiccated rites now faintly visible in peasant customs. The folklorist could reconstruct their original full-fleshed shapes, and the pre-historic world in which they functioned, by close comparisons with the myths of primitive peoples.

These bodies of living myths further explained to the folklorist the irrational elements in myths of civilized peoples. Lang puzzled over the question why classical Greece preserved in her mythology such barbarous ideas, and found his answer in the new anthropology of E. B. Tylor. Greek myths were survivals and distorted mirrors of an earlier culture when cannibalism and human sacrifice did indeed prevail. To see such customs intact in his own day, the folklorist needs simply turn to the Andaman Islanders, the African Hottentots, the Australian Noongahburrahs, and similar newly exposed areas of primitive life. Now the ugly Greek myth of Cronus becomes meaningful. Cronus cruelly castrated his father Uranus, who was about to embrace his mother Gaea. A Maori myth from New Zealand gives the key, depicting Heaven and Earth as a wedded couple, Heaven lying on Earth and imprisoning their children between them. Finally one child, the forest god, forces them asunder, freeing the offspring for their godly duties over the various elements. So did Cronus secure the separation of Heaven (Uranus) and Earth (Gaea), although the Hellenic Greeks had forgotten the original sense of the nature myth.[1]

Behind this method of folklore inquiry lay an enticing theory, transferred from Darwin's biology to the young science of anthropology and thence to folklore. Lang and his co-workers, G. L. Gomme, E. S. Hartland, and Edward Clodd, all accepted the unilinear view of cultural evolution. Mankind had climbed from his simian ancestry upward to the state of polished civilization by successive stages. All peoples ascended the evolutionary ladder in exactly the same manner. The savages of today were the Victorians of tomorrow, simply arrested by local circumstance, and conversely the Victorians of the contemporary moment were the savages of yesteryear.

In his far-reaching study of *The Legend of Perseus* (three volumes, 1894-1896), Edwin Sidney Hartland engaged upon the most sweeping application of the folklore method to a single classical myth. By slicing the Perseus myth into component episodes, such as the notions of the Supernatural Birth, the Life Token, the Witch and her Evil Eye, and pursuing their appearances throughout the world-wide collections of fairy tales, sagas, and savage mythologies, Hartland was able to demonstrate the substratum of primitive ideas underlying the literary myth. In the refined versions by Ovid and Strabo, Pausanias and Lucian, coarse traits essential to the primitive saga had dropped out: the external soul of the ogre, the lousing of the sleeping hero by his maiden-lover.

Another leading member of the anthropological school, Edward Clodd, examined the relationship between myth and the new study of folklore in his *Myths and Dreams* (1885).[2] The title of a preliminary lecture expresses more completely his point of view: "The Birth and Growth of Myth, and its Survival in Folk-Lore, Legend, and Dogma." Clodd saw in the concept of "myth" not merely the label for a narrative of the gods or the creation of the universe, but also the designation of an entire period in the stage of man's intellectual development, "a necessary travailing through which the mind of man passed in its slow progress towards certitude."[3] In this stage, prehistoric man corresponded to the child, taking dreams for reality, endowing inanimate objects with life, crediting animals with the power of speech.

While the anthropological school of folklorists depended on myths, in this broad sense, to document their major hypotheses, they were at the same time vigorously battling a rival group of myth interpreters. The philological school of comparative mythology, championed in England by Max Müller, unlocked the secrets of myths with the new key of Vedic Sanskrit. In his famous essay on *Comparative Mythology* in 1856, Müller outlined the principles governing the proper explication of myths. All Aryan tongues stemmed from the Sanskrit, which transferred to its offspring the names of gods, all referring to celestial phenomena. The basic equation lay in Dyaus = Zeus, uniting the two chief gods of the Vedic and Hellenic pantheons. Through a "disease of language," the original meanings and myths of the inherited names were forgotten and barbarous new myths arose to take their place. These myths had revolved around the sky (Dyaus) and the sun, the dawn and the clouds, and now comparative mythology could reconstruct these primary meanings buried within revolting Aryan mythologies.

So did solar mythology make its persuasive plea. Among the solarists who followed Müller's lead, George Cox outstripped all others in the sweep of his claims. Every mythical hero—from Herakles, Perseus, Theseus, Oedipus, Samson, down to Beowulf and King Arthur and the humbler heroes and heroines of the fairy tales, the Frog Prince, Cinderella, Hansel and Gretel—embodied the same solar deity or children of the dawn. One plot underlay all the primary myths and fairy tales, from the siege of Troy to the Song of Roland, the struggle of the sun against the powers of darkness. The sun hero battled monsters and ogres and armies, and suffered frightful trials in the nether regions, just as the sun toiled his way across the sky in the face of clouds and tempests. The gold he found at the end of his quest was the golden sunlight, and his magic swords, spears, and arrows were the sun's darting rays. All mythology revolved around the conflict between day and night.

The science of comparative mythology thus strove to incorporate into its system the narrative traditions prized by the folklorists. In leading the counterattack, Lang called repeated attention to the inner disagreements among the celestial mythologists. Müller read the dawn into his Sanskrit etymologies; others deciphered the storm, fire, the sky, raindrops, the moon. Who was right? The anthropologists also employed the weapon of ridicule, showing how readily "A Song of Sixpence" could be interpreted as solar myth: the pie is the earth, the crust the sky, the four and twenty blackbirds the hours; the king is the sun, and his money the golden sunshine.[4]

By the turn of the century the solar mythologists were

fairly routed. Four years after George Cox's *An Introduction
to the Science of Comparative Mythology and Folklore,* there
appeared in 1885 a rival volume faithfully presenting the
anthropological point of view, *An Introduction to Folk-Lore,*
by Marian Roalfe Cox, whose study of Cinderella constituted
the first extensive comparative investigation of a folk tale.
The anthropological school controlled the Folk-Lore Society
and dominated its publications during the remaining years
of "the great team of English folklorists." [5]

Half a century following the elaboration of Müller's theory
another symbolism descended on myth and sought to annex
folklore. The sun and the dawn yield to the son and the
mother. A new dispensation, Freud's *Interpretation of
Dreams,* replaces Müller's *Comparative Mythology,* and psychoanalysis succeeds philology as the handmaiden of myth,
laying bare the secret lore of the unconscious, as Vedic Sanskrit had opened the ancient wisdom of the East. Oedipus
now leads the pantheon, embracing Jocasta as heaven had
formerly clutched earth. In the myths, the toiling sun and
the darksome night abandon their ceaseless contention, giving way to the energetic phallus and the enveloping womb.
Where light had vanquished darkness, now, in the words of
Jung, consciousness triumphed over unconsciousness.[6] In the
specific terms of Freud, the hero is a wish fulfillment, and
the Devil personifies the "repressed unconscious instinctual
life." [7] No longer are the meanings of the myths writ large
in external, visible nature, but rather they are sunk deep in
man's unfathomed inner nature.

The Viennese psychoanalytical school could scarcely have
avoided familiarity with the German nature mythologists,
and the extent of their reading is seen in Otto Rank's study
of *The Myth of the Birth of the Hero.* Rank cites a shelfful
of writings by the older school, disparaging them but adopt-
ing their method of interpretation. Only the symbols change.
How transparent the myth of Cronus now is! [8] And how appropriate that the word "incest" comes from the Sanskrit! [9]

In Rank's gallery of heroes, the Freudian symbols fall
neatly into place. The myth hero corresponds to the child
ego, rebelling against the parents. The hostile father, pro-
jecting back his son's hatred, exposes the child in a box or

basket in the water; the box is the womb, and exposure in water is known in dreams to signalize birth. (The Flood myths are thus the hero myth amplified; the Ark is the box-womb.) The fact that birth has already occurred in the myth-story is easily explained away by Freud, who finds natural acts and fantasies from the unconscious peacefully succeeding each other in dream-myths. So the mythmakers are reconstructing their own childhood fantasies. The myth proves to be the delusion of a paranoiac resenting his father, who has pre-empted the mother's love.

Dreams, myths, and fairy tales tell one common story, a genital-anal saga. Thread is semen, wheat is the penis, salt is urine, gold is feces.[10] Defecation is itself symbolic of sub-limated or rejected sexuality. "Jack and the Beanstalk" was once a pleasant lunar myth-tale, with the moon as the bean of abundance which Jack climbs to the wealth of the morning light. Now it is a masturbation fantasy, in which the beans and the stalk symbolize testicles and penis.[11] Little Red Riding Hood, erstwhile a dawn maiden, has become a virgin ready for seduction; her red cap is a menstrual symbol, and her wandering in the woods a straying from the path of virtue; the wolf eating the girl is the sex act. But beyond this simple and obvious symbolism, Fromm finds subtler meanings, a "pregnancy envy" shown by the wolf (man), who fills his belly (womb) with the living grandmother and the girl, and is properly punished when Little Red Riding Hood stows stones, the symbol of sterility, in his insides. This copulation drama turns out to be a tale of women who hate men and sex.[12]

Just as the celestial mythologists wrangled over the primacy of sun, storms, and stars, so now do the psychoanalytical mythologists dispute over the symbols from the unconscious. Formerly it was Müller, Kuhn, Preller, Goldziher, Frobenius, who recriminated; now it is Freud, Jung, Ferenczi, Fromm, Kerényi, Róheim, Reik. The shifts and twistings of symbolism can be seen clearly enough in the crucial figure of Oedipus. In the solar orthodoxy of Cox, Oedipus the sun hero defeated the schemings of the thundercloud Sphinx that hung threateningly over the city of Thebes; he reunited with his mother Jocasta, the Dawn, from whom he had been parted since infancy; unwilling to see the misery he had wrought, he tore out his eyes, meaning that the sun had blinded himself in clouds and darkness; his death in the sanctuary of the Eumenides was the demise of the sun in the Groves of the Dawn, "the fairy network of clouds which are the first to receive and the last to lose the light of the sun in the morning and the evening." [13] Oedipus was hurried irresistibly on his predestined course, just as the sun journeyed compulsively onward.

In his revelation of the Oedipus complex Freud disclosed the wish fulfillment of our childhood goals, to sleep with our mothers and kill our fathers. Yet already in 1912, twelve years later, Ferenczi has added adornments. True both to Freud and to the older philological mythologists, he accepts Oedipus as the phallus, derived from the Greek "swell-foot"; the foot in dreams and jokes symbolizes the penis, and swelling signifies erection. But Ferenczi also worked in the castration complex, represented in Oedipus' blinding himself. The eyes, as paired organs, symbolize the testicles. Oedipus mutilated himself to express horror at his mother-incest, and also to avoid looking his father in the eye. Ferenczi reads this additional motive in the reply of Oedipus to the appalled Chorus, that Apollo fills his measure of woe. Apollo, the sun, is the father symbol. Hence Oedipus, formerly the sun hero, is now son of the sun god, and thus, if both readings are accepted, has become his own father. [14]

Erich Fromm shifted the burden to a conflict between matriarchy and patriarchy, revealed in the whole Oedipus trilogy, with Oedipus, Haemon, and Antigone upholding the matriarchal order against the tyranny of Creon. Fittingly Oedipus dies in the grove of the matriarchal goddesses, to whose world he belongs. Jung, moving farther afield, is bitterly castigated by Freud for exciding the libido from the Oedipus complex, and substituting for the erotic impulses an ethical conflict between the "life task" that lies ahead and the "psychic laziness" that holds one back, clinging to the skirts of an idealized mother and a self-centered father. [15]

Fairy tales, regarded by the mythologists as truncated myths, occasion the same discords. When Müller solarized "The Frog King," first of the Grimms' *Kinder- und Haus-*

märchen, he saw the frog as one more name for the sun, and worked out a derivation from the Sanskrit. People in the mythopoeic age called the frog the sun when they saw it squatting on the water. Ernest Jones, the voice of Freud, recognizes the frog as the penis. So the unconscious regards the male organ in moments of disgust, and the fairy-tale moral is the gradual overcoming of the maiden's aversion to the sex act. In the chaster, archetypal reading of Jung, according to Joseph Campbell, the frog is a miniature dragon-serpent, loathsome in appearance but representing the "unconscious deep" filled with hidden treasures. He is the herald summoning forth the child from her infantile world to the land of adventure, independence, maturity, self-discovery, and at the same time filling her with anxiety at the thought of separation from her mother. Her golden ball lost in the well is the sun, the deep dark spring waters suggest the night; so the older symbolism overlays the newer.[16]

Even in their joint commentaries on the Winnebago trickster, the contemporary mythologists differ. Kerényi sees the ubiquitous Indian scapegrace and culture hero as the phallus; Jung and Radin find in him god, man, woman, animal, buffoon, hero, the amalgam of opposites, the reflection of both consciousness and unconsciousness.[17]

Toward the new symbolism of the psychoanalytical schools, the folklorist of today takes a position similar to that held by Lang and his fellows of yesterday. The language of the unconscious is as conjectural and inconclusive as Sanskrit, when applied to myths and tales. The tortured interpretations differ widely from each other; which is right? The psychoanalysts, like the philologists, come to the materials of folklore from the outside, anxious to exploit them for their own a priori assumptions. The folklorist begins with the raw data of his field and sees where they lead him. He can admire the symmetrical structure reared by Joseph Campbell from many disparate materials, but the folk literatures that occupy him cannot all be prettily channeled into the universal monomyth.[18] The issue between contemporary mythologists and folklorists has, however, never been joined, because the one subject they could have debated, myth, has dropped from the vocabulary of folklore.

The English anthropological school of folklore did not long enjoy their conquest of the solar mythologists. Their own theory of survivals soon collapsed before the detailed field inquiries of modern anthropology.[19] Leadership in folklore studies passed to the Continent, centering in the historical-geographical technique of the Finnish scholars. Collecting, archiving, and the comparative study of branching variants became, and still are, the order of the day. In the United States a division of labor has resulted between humanistic folklorists, who would abandon the term "myth," and cultural anthropologists, who would discard the term "folklore."[20] It is no accident that the keenest review of current theories of myth has been provided by the anthropologists Melville and Frances Herskovits, who test them empirically against their field materials.[21] The collectors of folk traditions in contemporary America encounter almost all forms of traditional narrative—legend, anecdote, ghost story, *Märchen,* animal tale, jest, dialect story, tall tale, dirty joke, cante-fable—save only myth. The word "myth" is still flourished, say, at the mention of Davy Crockett or Paul Bunyan, but in the same fuzzy sense indistinguishable in common usage from "legend" or "folklore."[22] Cultural historians like Henry Nash Smith or Richard Hofstadter employ "myth" with the quite separate meaning of a popularly accepted cluster of images.[23]

The progress of field collecting shows that mythologists and folklorists are dealing with different classes of material. In writing on Greek gods and heroes, Kerényi prefers sacred myths of the priests and poets to the heroic saga of the folk. The folklorist exhibits just the opposite preference. Heroic saga is the very stuff of folk tradition, and the Chadwicks in their exhaustive studies have explained the formation of folk epics in terms eminently sensible to the folklorists.[24] The hero is not the sun, or the penis, or superconsciousness, but a great warrior around whom legends gather. The gold he wins is neither sunlight nor dung, but the same legendary gold that inspires countless treasure quests in real life, among down-East lobstermen, Southern Negroes, and Western cowhands.

The Crockett tradition follows in detail after detail the

Chadwicks' analysis, even given the special conditions of American history. From the frontier setting issues a Heroic Age society; Crockett is the historical figure to whom oral and written legends fasten; he undergoes adventures similar to those of all folk-epic heroes—single combats, wanderings, love affairs. He possesses famed weapons, utters fierce boasts, displays precocious strength, and meets death against great odds, like the other Heroic Age champions. His printed tales, close to their oral substratum, reveal him as a clownish hero, again in keeping with the Chadwicks' findings, but the first step in the literary process leading to epic dignity can be seen in the almanac embroidery of the tradition.[25]

The recent Disney-inspired revival of Crockett had nothing to do with the folk figure, but like the Paul Bunyan story was packaged by the mass media for popular consumption. These assembly-line demigods, numbering now nearly a dozen, belong to the "folklore of industrial man," as Marshall McLuhan has called it in *The Mechanical Bride,* discussing themes that are not folklore at all but "pop kutch." At the bottom of the Paul Bunyan fanfare lies the slenderest trickle of oral taletelling, and this has vanished in the sands of journalistic, advertising, radio, and juvenile-book regurgitation of Bunyan antics. Paul Bunyan has entered the vocabulary of journalism as a convenient humorous symbol for mammoth size and gargantuan undertakings, but the readings of the symbol vary widely. The lumber industry sees in him the exemplar of giant production, the *Daily Worker* finds in him the spirit of the workingman, artists extract from him the sheer brute strength of the American genius, resort promoters exhibit a big dummy to attract tourists.[26]

A recent essay claims that the rebellious youth-idol hero, a composite of Marlon Brando, James Dean, and Elvis Presley, is the lineal descendant of Crockett and Bunyan. There can be no direct connection between a hero of oral folk tradition and the idol of teen-age mass adoration, but as mass-culture heroes, Crockett and Brando shocking the dudes, Superman and James Dean hurtling through space, Tarzan and Elvis Presley grunting and grimacing, do have an affinity.[27]

Also in the domain of "pop kutch" belong the Paul Bunyan-sized treasuries of "folklore," assembled most vigorously by Benjamin A. Botkin. These bargain packages use folklore as a bright label for their miscellany of local gags, schmalz, nostalgic reminiscences, and journalistic jokes, clipped from second-hand sources, with all coarse and obscene elements excluded, and a wide geographical area covered, to insure large distribution. There is a bit of sentiment and fun for everybody in these BIG American albums.

The problems in American folklore studies today are to separate the folklore of the folk from the fake lore of industrial man, and to establish among many specialists a common ground based on the unique circumstances of American history. There is a need to secure general acceptance of scholarly procedures in collecting and reporting the raw materials of folklore. In these respects American folklorists have a good deal of catching up to do to reach the solid platform of their English predecessors. The question of myth is far afield. But when it is posed, the lesson taught by Andrew Lang still holds, and the folklorist looks with a jaundiced eye at the excessive strainings of mythologists to extort symbols from folk tales.

NOTES

[1] Andrew Lang, "The Myth of Cronus," in *Custom and Myth* (London, 1901), pp. 45-63.

[2] London, published by the Sunday Lecture Society, 1875.

[3] *Myths and Dreams* (London, 1891), pp. 5-6.

[4] E. B. Tylor, *Primitive Culture* (3rd edn., London, 1891), Vol. I, p. 319.

[5] As I have described them in an article of that title in the *Journal of American Folklore*, LXIV (1951), pp. 1-10. My discussion of the Lang-Müller controversy, "The Eclipse of Solor Mythology," appeared in the same journal, LXVIII (1955), pp. 393-416, in a special symposium on myth, edited by Thomas A. Sebeok. Titled *Myth: A Symposium*, this group of papers also appears as Volume 5 in the Bibliographical and Special Series of the American Folklore Society (Philadelphia, 1955), and has been reprinted by the Indiana University Press (Bloomington, Indiana, 1958).

[6] C. G. Jung and C. Kerényi, *Essays on a Science of Mythology*, trans. R. F. C. Hull (New York: Pantheon Books, 1949), p. 119.

[7] *The Interpretation of Dreams*, in *The Basic Writings of Sigmund Freud*, trans. and ed. A. A. Brill (New York: The Modern Library, 1938), p. 308; S. Freud and D. E. Oppenheim, *Dreams in Folklore*, trans. A. M. O. Richards (New York: International Universities Press, 1958), p. 39.

8 Otto Rank, *The Myth of the Birth of the Hero, A Psychological Interpretation of Mythology,* trans. F. Robbins and S. E. Jelliffe (New York: Robert Brunner, 1952, 2nd ed. 1957), p. 93, note 97.

9 Ernest Jones, *Essays in Applied Psycho-Analysis,* Vol. II, "Essays in Folklore, Anthropology and Religion" (London: Hogarth Press, 1951), p. 19.

10 See, e.g., Jones, "The Symbolic Significance of Salt," *ibid.,* pp. 22-109; Freud and Oppenheim, "Feces Symbolism and Related Dream Actions," *op. cit.,* pp. 36-65.

11 Angelo de Gubernatis, *Zoological Mythology* (2 vols., New York and London, 1872), Vol. I, p. 244; William H. Desmonde, "Jack and the Beanstalk," *American Imago,* VIII (1951), pp. 287-288.

12 Erich Fromm, *The Forgotten Language, An Introduction to the Understanding of Dreams, Fairy Tales and Myths* (New York: Rinehart & Co., 1951), pp. 235-241.

13 George W. Cox, *An Introduction to the Science of Comparative Mythology and Folklore* (London, 1881), p. 126.

14 Freud, *The Interpretation of Dreams,* in *The Basic Writings of Sigmund Freud* (New York: The Modern Library, 1938), pp. 307-309; Sándor Ferenczi, "The Symbolic Representation of the Pleasure and the Reality Principles in the Oedipus Myth," *Imago,* I, 1912, reprinted in *Sex in Psychoanalysis,* trans. Ernest Jones (New York: Robert Brunner, 1950), pp. 253-269.

15 Fromm, "The Oedipus Myth," in *The Forgotten Language,* pp. 196-231; Freud, *The History of the Psychoanalytic Movement,* in *The Basic Writings of Sigmund Freud,* p. 974. Rival psychoanalytic systems are considered in Patrick Mullahy, *Oedipus, Myth and Complex* (New York, 1948; reprinted in Evergreen Edition, 1955).

16 Max Müller, *Chips from a German Workshop* (New York, 1872), Vol. II, pp. 244-246; Ernest Jones, "Psycho-Analysis and Folklore," *op. cit.,* Vol. II, p. 16; Joseph Campbell, *The Hero with a Thousand Faces* (New York: Pantheon Books, 1949), pp. 49-53.

17 Paul Radin, *The Trickster, A Study in American Indian Mythology,* with commentaries by Karl Kerényi and C. G. Jung (New York: Philosophical Library, 1956). Cf. Kerényi pp. 183-185, with Radin, p. 169, and Jung, p. 203.

18 Joseph Campbell's achievement in *The Hero with a Thousand Faces* rests on equal familiarity with folklore, psychoanalysis, literature, and theology. His brilliantly written "Folkloristic Commentary" to the Pantheon Books edition of *Grimm's Fairy Tales* (New York, 1944), pp. 833-864, shows his mastery of folk-tale scholarship.

19 The psychoanalytical mythologists evinced considerable interest in the survival theory. Freud saw the savage as well as the child in adult dreams and neuroses (Ernest Jones, *The Life and Work of Sigmund Freud,* Vol. II, New York: Basic Books, Inc., 1955,

p. 272), and made elaborate analogies bteween savages and neurotics in *Totem and Taboo.* Speaking at a congress of the English Folklore Society, Ernest Jones referred to "survivals" in the individual unconscious of totemistic beliefs, corresponding to survivals in racial memory ("Psycho-Analysis and Folklore," p. 7).

20 Stith Thompson, "Myths and Folktales," in *Myth: A Symposium,* pp. 482-488; William R. Bascom, "Verbal Art," *Journal of American Folklore,* LXVIII (1955), pp. 245-252.

21 Melville J. and Frances S. Herskovits, "A Cross-Cultural Approach to Myth," in *Dahomean Narrative* (Evanston, Ill.: Northwestern University Press, 1958), pp. 81-122. See also the review by M. J. Herskovits of Fromm, *The Forgotten Language,* in *Journal of American Folklore,* LXVI (1953), pp. 87-89.

22 E.g., Stuart A. Stiffler, "Davy Crockett: The Genesis of Heroic Myth," *Tennessee Historical Quarterly,* XVI (1957), pp. 134-140.

23 Thus H. N. Smith, *Virgin Land, The American West as Symbol and Myth* (Cambridge, Mass.: Harvard University Press, 1950); R. Hofstadter, "The Agrarian Myth and Commercial Realities," in *The Age of Reform* (New York: Alfred A. Knopf, Inc., 1956), pp. 23-59.

24 C. Kerényi, *The Gods of the Greeks* (London and New York: Thames & Hudson, 1951); H. M. and N. K. Chadwick, *The Growth of Literature* (3 vols., Cambridge: Cambridge University Press, 1932-1940).

25 I developed this idea in "Davy Crockett and the Heroic Age," *Southern Folklore Quarterly,* VI (1942), pp. 95-102.

26 My evidence for the journalistic treatment of Bunyan is given in "Paul Bunyan in the News, 1939-1941," *Western Folklore,* XV (1956), pp. 26-39, 179-193, 247-261. The only full scholarly treatment is by Daniel G. Hoffman, *Paul Bunyan, Last of the Frontier Demi-Gods* (Philadelphia: University of Pennsylvania Press, 1952).

27 Robert S. Brustein, "America's New Culture Hero," *Commentary,* XXV (February 1958), pp. 123-129. Leo Gurko considers the musclebound quality of American mass heroes in "Folklore of the American Hero," in *Heroes, Highbrows and the Popular Mind* (Indianapolis and New York: Bobbs-Merrill Co., 1953), pp. 168-198.

SUGGESTIONS FOR DISCUSSION

1. Does Dorson object to sexual or solar interpretations of myth *per se?* Does his view make myths easier for the layman to understand than do the views of the psychoanalysts and the philologists? What special equipment is necessary, according to him, for the interpreter of myth?
2. Dorson makes a distinction between sacred myth and heroic saga: why might Murray object to the separation? What advantages and disadvantages are there, in your opinion, to the two views?
3. Why does Dorson not consider the traditional Crockett legend a

myth? The recent accumulations of Crockett lore? The Paul Bunyan story? The cluster of Brando-Dean-Presley legends?

4. Does the fact that a legend circulates by means of the mass media seem a good reason for barring it from the category of myth? Would Murray's definitions encompass these tales?

5. What evidence do you find that Dorson, Murray, and the psycho-analyst work from different presuppositions about the human imag-ination—about the extent to which it varies from place to place and from age to age?

RECURRENT THEMES IN MYTHS
AND MYTHMAKING

CLYDE KLUCKHOHN

It is the purpose of this paper to draw together some information on and interpretation of certain features of mythology that are apparently universal or that have such wide distribution in space and time that their generality may be presumed to result from recurrent reactions of the human psyche to situations and stimuli of the same general order. Addressing a group from a wide range of disciplinary affiliations, I shall utilize recent writings that are, as yet, generally familiar only to anthropologists and folklorists. I shall also add a modest effort on my own part to sample independently the distribution of a small number of mythic elements. The result makes no pretensions to completeness or indeed to more than approximate accuracy on the materials surveyed. But even a crude and tentative synthesis may have some inter-

---

CLYDE KLUCKHOHN, born in Le Mars, Iowa, in 1905, was chairman of the Department of Anthropology at Harvard University. He was director of the Russian Research Center at Harvard from 1947 to 1954. During World War II he served as Cochief of the Joint Morale Survey (Military Intelligence Service and Office of War Information). In the postwar years he was a consultant to various government agencies. His books include *The Navaho* (with D. C. Leighton); *Mirror for Man;* and *How the Soviet System Works* (with R. Bauer and A. Inkeles). He died in 1960.

est and provide some stimulation to more comprehensive and precise research.

Literary scholars, psychiatrists, and behavioral scientists have, of course, long recognized that diverse geographical areas and historical epochs have exhibited striking parallels in the themes of myth and folklore. Father-seekers and father-slayers appear again and again. Mother-murder appears in explicit and in disguised form (see Bunker, 1944). Eliade (1949) has dealt with the myth of "the eternal return." Marie Bonaparte (1947) has presented evidence that wars give rise to fantasies of patently similar content. Animal stories—at least in the Old World—show likenesses in many details of plot and embellishment: African tales and Reynard the Fox, the Aesop fables, the Panchatantra of India and the Jataka tales of China (see Herskovits and Herskovits, 1958, p. 118). The Orpheus story has a sizable distribution in the New World (Gayton, 1935).

In considering various parallels, some elementary cautions must perforce be observed. First, levels of abstraction must be kept distinct. It is true, and it is relevant, to say that creation myths are universals or near-universals. But this is a far more abstract statement than are generalizations about the frequency of the creation of human beings by mother earth and father sky, or by an androgynous deity, or from vegetables. Second, mere comparisons on the basis of the presence or absence of a trait are tricky and may well be misleading. Although there are cases where I have as yet no positive evidence for the presence of the incest theme, there is no corpus of mythology that I have searched carefully where this motif does not turn up. Even if, however, incest could be demonstrated as a theme present in all mythologies, there would still be an important difference between mythologies preoccupied with incest and those where it occurs only incidentally and infrequently. Nevertheless, the methodological complications of reliable ratings upon the centrality or strength of a given theme are such that in this paper I must deal almost exclusively with sheer presence or absence.

Most anthropologists today would agree with Lévi-Strauss (1955) that throughout the world myths resemble one another to an extraordinary degree; there is, indeed, an "astounding similarity between myths collected in widely different regions." The differences are there too, of course, between cultures and culture areas, even between versions of "the same" myth collected on the same day from two or more individuals of a particular culture. Some myths appear to have a very limited geographical distribution; other themes that have a very wide or perhaps universal distribution are varyingly styled, weighted, and combined. These differences are very real and very massive, and there must be no tacit attempt to explain them away. For some purposes of inquiry the focus must be upon questions of emphasis, of inversion of plot, of selective omission and addition, of reinterpretation, of every form of variation. The similarities, however, are also genuine, and it is upon these that I shall concentrate. After all, presumably no two events in the universe are literally identical. But there are formal resemblances at varying levels of abstraction that are interesting and significant.

Let us begin with some broad universals. I have already mentioned the creation myth.[1] This may seem so broad a category as to be empty. Yet Rooth (1957) on analyzing three hundred creation myths of the North American Indians finds that most of them fit comfortably into eight types and that seven of these types appear likewise in Eurasia. She interprets the similarities in types and in congruence of detail motifs between North America and Eurasia (and also some between Peru, Meso-America, and the Pacific Islands) as due to historic diffusion. Were this inference to be demonstrated as valid in all respects, there would still remain the fact that these plots and their details had sufficient psychological meaning to be preserved through the centuries.

There are two ways of reasoning that bulk prominently in all mythological systems. These are what Sir James Frazer called the "laws" of sympathetic magic (like causes like) and holophrastic magic (the part stands for the whole). These principles are particularly employed in one content area where the record is so full and so exceptionless that we are justified in speaking of genuine cultural universals. I know of no culture without myths and tales relating to witchcraft, and the following themes seem to appear always and everywhere.

1. Were-animals who move about at night with miraculous speed, gathering in witches' sabbaths to work evil magic.
2. The notion that illness, emaciation, and eventual death can result from introducing by magical means some sort of noxious substance into the body of the victim.
3. A connection between incest and witchcraft.

So far as I have been able to discover, the only cultural variability here concerns minutiae: details of the magical techniques; which animals are portrayed; what kinds of particles are shot into the victim or what kinds of witchcraft poisons are employed. It is, to be sure, conceivable that once again we are dealing with diffusion: that all known cultures derive eventually from a generalized Paleolithic culture in which these items of witchcraft lore were already evolved. But, again, their persistence cannot be understood except on the hypothesis that these images have a special congeniality for the human mind as a consequence of the relations of children to their parents and other childhood experiences which are universal rather than culture-bound.

While a comprehensive interpretation of any myth or of mythologies must rest upon the way in which themes are combined—upon, as Lévi-Strauss (1955, 1957) says, "a bundle of features"—nevertheless the mere recurrence of certain motifs in varied areas separated geographically and historically tells us something about the human psyche. It suggests that the interaction of a certain kind of biological apparatus in a certain kind of physical world with some inevitables of the human condition (the helplessness of infants, two parents of different sex, etc.) bring about some regularities in the formation of imaginative productions, of powerful images. I want to consider examples of these, only mentioning some but discussing others at a little greater length. I have selected themes that have been stated by various students of comparative mythology to be nearly universal in distribution.

In most cases we cannot say strictly that these images are universal, either because of incomplete evidence or because of known exceptions, but we can say that some are known from all or almost all of the major culture areas of the world. To avoid egregious sampling errors and generally to make the inquiry more systematic, I have used Murdock's (1957) "world ethnographic sample." He presents a carefully selected sample of all the cultures known to history and ethnography, classified into sixty culture areas. Richard Moench and I tried to cover one culture from each of these areas but were able to work through only fifty—and this not exhaustively. The fifty are, however, distributed about evenly among Murdock's six major regions (Circum-Mediterranean, Negro Africa, East Eurasia, Insular Pacific, North America, South America). To the extent that time permitted, we used standard monographic sources on the cultures in question (or excerpts from these sources in the Human Relations Area Files at Harvard). We also had recourse to certain compendia: the Hastings *Encyclopaedia of Religion and Ethics, Myths of All Races,* Stith Thompson's *Motif Index,* and others.

Our results are far from satisfactory, but they do represent a start. On the positive side, they ought to be almost completely trustworthy. That is, where we report, for eample, that brother-sister incest is a mythological theme in Micronesia, this can be regarded as established. It is on the negative side that doubt must be raised. For instance, we did not discover an androgynous deity in the mythology of the Warrau. This, unfortunately, does not necessarily mean that no such deity exists in Warrau mythology—only that we discovered no reference in the one original source and in the compilations we checked. Without question, a more intensive search than we were able to conduct would enlarge—we cannot guess by how great a factor—the number of features to be tabulated as "present."

Flood. We found this theme—usually, but not always, treated as a punishment—in thirty-four of our fifty mythologies. The distribution is not far from equal in five of the six regions, but we encountered only one reference from Negro Africa. There is the possibility that some of these tales take their ultimate source from the mythology of the Near East and, specifically, Jewish-Christian mythology, although many ethnographers are careful to discriminate explicitly between those that may have this derivation and others that seem definitely "aboriginal." Li Hwei (see Bascom, 1957, p. 114) has traced fifty-one flood myths in Formosa, South China,

Southeast Asia, and Malaysia that it hardly seems plausible to attribute to Jewish-Christian sources.[2] At any rate, if one adds earthquakes, famines, plagues, etc., it is likely, on present evidence, that "catastrophe" can be considered as a universal or near-universal theme in mythology.

Slaying of Monsters. This theme appears in thirty-seven of our fifty cultures, and here the distribution approaches equality save for a slightly greater frequency in North America and the Insular Pacific. Not infrequently, the elaboration of the theme has a faintly Oedipal flavor. Thus in Bantu Africa (and beyond) a hero is born to a woman who survives after a monster has eaten her spouse (and everyone else). The son immediately turns into a man, slays a monster or monsters, restores his people—but not his father—and becomes chief.

Incest. This is overtly depicted in thirty-nine mythologies. In three cases (Celtic, Greek, and Hindu) mother-son, father-daughter, and brother-sister incest are alluded to; eleven cases mention two forms of incest; the remaining twenty-five mythologies apparently deal with only a single type. In our sample we encountered only seven references to mother-son incest (none in Negro Africa and only one in East Eurasia). In other reading we did find an additional seven reports—one more from East Eurasia but still none from Negro Africa. Brother-sister incest was easily the most popular theme in the sample (twenty-eight cases). There are twelve cases of father-daughter incest. In creation stories, the first parents are not infrequently depicted as incestuous, and there are numerous references to the seduction of a mother-in-law by her son-in-law (or vice versa).

Sibling Rivalry. We discovered thirty-two instances of this theme, which appears from all six "continental" regions but —so far as our sample goes—is appreciably more frequent in the Insular Pacific and in Negro Africa. The rivalry between brothers is portrayed far oftener than any other, and usually in the form of fratricide. There were only four cases of brother-sister quarrels (one resulting in murder) and only two of sister-sister. There are some indications in the data that a larger sample and a finer analysis would reveal some culturally distinctive regularities as regards the age order of siblings depicted as rivalrous. For example, in parts of Negro

Africa it appears that it is always two siblings born in immediate sequence who are chosen as protagonists.

Castration. We found only four cases where actual castration is mentioned in the myths, and one of these (Trobriand)
is self-inflicted castration, ostensibly as a reaction to guilt
over adultery. There were in addition five cases in which the
threat of castration to boys is mentioned in myths as a social-
ization technique. There are also instances (e.g., Baiga) where
there are reports of severed penes and injured testicles. However, if one counts themes of "symbolic castration," then
there is an approach toward universality. The subincision
rites of the Australian aborigines have been so interpreted.
And in our browsing (beyond our sample) we encountered
the *vagina dentata* motif among the following peoples: Arap-
aho, Bellabella, Bellacoola, Blackfoot, Comox, Coos, Crow,
Dakota, Iroquois, Jicarilla, Kwakiutl, Maidu, Nez Percé,
Pawnee, San Carlos Apache, Shoshone, Shuswap, Thompson,
Tsimshian, Walapai, Wichita; Ainu; Samoa; Naga; Kiwai
Papuan.

Androgynous Deities. From our sample we can document
only seven cases (all from Circum-Mediterranean, East Eurasia, and North America). Eliade (1958[a], p. 25) says that divine
bisexuality is not found "in really primitive religions." The
numerous examples he gives (1958[b], pp. 420-425) are all from
"advanced" religions, though we could add a few from "primitive" cultures.

OEDIPUS-TYPE MYTHS

Let us now turn to a brief examination of two patterns in
which themes are combined. The Oedipus story has long
haunted European literature and thought, even if in very recent times the myth of Sisyphus may have replaced that of
Oedipus in popularity (see Kafka, Camus, and many others).
Jones (1954) has tried to show that *Hamlet* is basically an
Oedipal plot. Others insist that Great Mother or Mater Dolo-
rosa tales are simply special variants.

At all events, some scholars have regarded the Oedipal tale
as prototypical of all human myths. Critical scrutiny of this
generalization, and particularly one's conclusions as to the
prevalence of Oedipus-type myths outside the areas the story

may have reached through historical diffusion, will rest on how much credence one is prepared to give to psychoanalytic interpretations of latent content, on the one hand; and on how many elements of the Greek myth one demands be replicated, on the other. Thus Róheim's (1950, pp. 319-347) contention that certain Navaho myths are Oedipal strikes many as strained. The main emphasis is upon the father killing his own children—even here Róheim must argue that it is the father's *weapon* that is used (by another). And he must contend that the giant who makes amorous advances to the mother and is killed by the sons is a *father substitute*.

Actually, the forty-eight Oedipal myths in the Euro-Asiatic area analyzed by Rank (1952) and Raglan (1956) do not show a very striking fit in detail (see Bascom, 1957) to the Greek myth. In only four of these does the hero marry his mother. Indeed, in only eight others is an incestuous theme of any kind explicitly present. Again, in only four of the forty-eight myths does the hero cause the death of his father. In nine other cases the hero kills (or in one case is killed by) a close relative (grandfather, uncle, brother, etc.). One can make a good case for "antagonism against close relatives—*usually* of the same sex" as a prominent motif, and a fair case for physical violence against such relatives. But neither parricide nor Raglan's regicide motifs will stand up literally without a great deal of farfetched interpretation.

In a very interesting paper Lessa (1956) has suggested that the Oedipus-type story spread by diffusion from the patriarchal Euro-Asiatic societies to Oceanic peoples with whom the situation is very different. He writes:

> ... We find such stories limited to a continuous belt extending from Europe to the Near and Middle East and southeastern Asia, and from there into the islands of the Pacific. It seems to be absent from such vast areas as Africa, China, central Asia, northeastern Asia, North America, South America, and Australia [page 68].

In an examination of several thousand Oceanic narratives Lessa found twenty-three that bore some resemblance to the Oedipus tale. He points out, however, that none meet all three of his major criteria [3] (prophecy, parricide, and incest) or his minor criteria (succorance from exposure, rearing by another king, fulfillment of prophecy); only a third meet the combination of parricide and incest. Lessa also calls attention to various "substitutions": mother's brother for father, father's sister for mother, son kills father rather than the other way round, incest merely threatened rather than consummated, baby abandoned but without hostility.

Nevertheless, even if one grants Lessa's inference of diffusion (with culturally appropriate substitutions), I do not think one can at present assent to his main argument without exception. Róheim's (1950) case for Oedipal pattern in the myths of Australian aborigines, Yurok, Navaho, and others does indeed involve too much reliance upon "unconscious ideas" and "real motifs." And yet, in my opinion, something remains that cannot altogether be explained away. Lessa asserts flatly that Oedipal tales are absent from Africa, but they are found among the Shilluk (Bascom, 1957, p. 111); and the Lamba (central Bantu) have a story of a son killing his father, in which there is a fairly overt motif of sexual rivalry for the mother.

Herskovits and Herskovits (1958, p. 94) make two significant points as regards testing generalizing conclusions about the Oedipus myth in cross-cultural perspective. The first (abundantly confirmed by the present small study) is neglect of rivalry between brothers. Then they say:

> In analyzing the motivating forces underlying the myth clusters that fall into the Oedipus category, we must take into account not only the son's jealousy of the father, but also the father's fear of being displaced by his son. Parent-child hostilities, that is, are not unidirectional. As manifest in myth, and in the situations of everyday experience, they are an expression of the broader phenomenon of intergenerational competition. These tensions, moreover, begin in infancy in the situation of rivalry between children of the same parents for a single goal, the attention of the mother. This rivalry sets up patterns of interaction that throughout life give rise to attitudes held toward the siblings or sibling substitutes with whom the individual was in competition during infancy, and it is our hypothesis that these attitudes are later projected by the father upon his offspring. In myth, if the psychological interpretation is to be granted validity, we must posit that the threat to the father or father-surrogate is to be seen as a projection of the infantile experience of sibling hostility upon the son. It may be

said to be the response to the reactivation of early attitudes toward the mother under the stimulus of anticipated competition for the affection of the wife.

The hypothesis that the main direction of hostility is from father to son received much confirmation from our reading from the following: fourteen North American peoples; four Circum-Mediterranean peoples; five from East Eurasia; three from the Insula Pacific; four from Africa. These were noted incidentally in searching for material on our selected themes. In many cases the myth states as an explicit motif the father's fear of being killed or displaced by his son. In some instances a prophecy is mentioned. Sometimes the son is expelled by the father rather than killed. An Azande father is depicted as destroying an incestuous son by magic. An Alor father orders his wife to kill the next child *if* male. There are many variants, but the basic theme is certainly a prevalent one.

THE MYTH OF THE HERO

It strikes me that the Oepidal pattern may best be considered as one form of a far more widespread myth, which has been treated by Rank (1952), Raglan (1956), and Campbell (1956). Rank abstracts the following pattern in thirty-four myths from the Mediterranean basin and western Asia:

The hero is the child of most distinguished parents; usually the son of a king. His origin is preceded by difficulties, such as continence, or prolonged barrenness or secret intercourse of the parents, due to external prohibition or obstacles. During the pregnancy, or antedating the same, there is a prophecy in the form of a dream or oracle, cautioning against his birth, and usually threatening danger to the father, or his representative. As a rule, he is surrendered to the water, in a box. He is then saved by animals, or lowly people (shepherds) and is suckled by a female animal, or by a humble woman. After he is grown up, he finds his distinguished parents in a highly versatile fashion; takes his revenge on his father, on the one hand, and is acknowledged on the other, and finally achieves rank and honors [page 61].

Raglan's first thirteen (of twenty-two) points correspond strikingly to this formula. In a world-wide context Campbell develops essentially the same pattern in a more sophisticated form, tied neither to the doctrinaire psychoanalysis of Rank nor to the limited and culture-bound theories of Raglan.

From the reading done by Moench and myself, many details not cited in any of the above three publications could be added: numerous instances of parricide in myth; virgin and other kinds of miraculous birth; newborn child in basket or pot; care of the infant by animals or humble women; and the like. This would, however, be more of the same fragmentary information. Rather, I shall add to the record two recent pertinent studies that are more systematic.

Ishida (1955) shows the prevalence in the Far East of all of this "bundle" of themes except prophecy. There are, of course, certain cultural embellishments that are characteristically different, but the plot is patently similar except for the omission of prophecy and the addition of a theme not present in the Rank formula: greater emphasis upon the mother of the hero, and often the worship of her along with her divine son.

But Ishida's research deals with the same continental land mass from which Rank and Raglan draw their data. Let us therefore take an example from the New World, Spencer's (1957, see especially pp. 19, 73) analysis of Navaho mythology. The following similarities may be noted:

1. These are also hero stories: adventures and achievements of extraordinary kind (e.g., slaying monsters, overcoming death, controlling the weather).
2. There is often something special about the birth of the hero (occasionally heroine).
3. Help from animals is a frequent motif.
4. A separation from one or both parents at an early age is involved.
5. There is antagonism and violence toward near kin, though mainly toward siblings or father-in-law. This hostility may be channeled in one or both directions. It may be masked but is more often expressed in violent acts.
6. There is eventual return and recognition with honor. The hero's achievements are realized by his immediate family, and redound in some way to their benefit and that of the larger group to which the family belongs.

Contrasts between the Old World and New World forms are clearly reflected in content and emphasis. The themes of social hierarchy and of triumph over (specifically) the father are absent in the American Indian version, and the Navaho theme of anxiety over subsistence is absent from the Euro-Asian plot. Yet at a broad psychological level the similarities are also impressive. In both cases we have a form of "family romance": the hero is separated but in the end returns in a high status; prohibitions and portents and animals play a role; there are two features of the Oedipus myth as Lévi-Strauss (1955) has "translated" it— "under-estimation and over-estimation of near kin."

Of constant tendencies in mythmaking, I shall merely remind you of four that are so well documented as to be unarguable, then mention two others:

1. Duplication, triplication, and quadruplication of elements. (Lévi-Strauss, 1955, suggests that the function of this repetition is to make the structure of the myth apparent.)
2. Reinterpretation of borrowed myths to fit pre-existing cultural emphases.
3. Endless variations upon central themes.
4. Involution-elaboration.

The psychoanalysts have maintained that mythmaking exemplifies a large number of the mechanisms of ego defense. I agree, and have provided examples from Navaho culture (Kluckhohn, 1942). Lévi-Strauss (1955, 1957) suggests that mythical thought always works from awareness of binary oppositions toward their progressive mediation. That is, the contribution of mythology is that of providing a logical model capable of overcoming contradictions in a people's view of the world and what they have deduced from their experience. This is an engaging idea, but much further empirical work is required to test it.

In conclusion, it may be said that this incomplete and exploratory study adds a small bit of confirmation to the finding of others that there are detectable trends toward regularities both in myths and in mythmaking. At least some themes and the linking of certain features of them, while differently stylized and incorporating varying detailed content according to culture and culture area, represent recurrent fantasies that have held the imaginations of many, if not most, social groups.

NOTES

1 Myths of the creation of the world are infrequent in some areas (e.g., Melanesia and Indonesia). But stories of the creation of mankind appear to be universal. Many themes recur in widely separated areas but do not approach universality: the first parents are sun and moon or earth and sky; the first impregnation comes from the rays of the sun; the first humans are fashioned from earth by a creator or emerge as vegetables from the earth and cannot at first walk straight. Destruction of an old world and creation of a new is likewise a frequently recurring story.

2 Lord Raglan (1956) relates the flood myth to the flooding of rivers and the whole problem of subsistence in newly agricultural civilizations. But it occurs in many nonliterate societies, including some that do not have even incipient agriculture.

3 Lessa's criteria are those of the Aarne-Thompson classification of folk tales.

REFERENCES

Bascom, William, "The Myth-Ritual Theory," *Journal of American Folklore,* 1957, *70:* 103-115.

Bonaparte, Marie, *Myths of War.* London: Imago Publishing Company, Ltd., 1947.

Bunker, H. A., "Mother-Murder in Myth and Legend," *Psychoanalytic Quarterly,* 1944, *13:* 198-207.

Campbell, Joseph, *The Hero with a Thousand Faces.* New York: Meridian Books, 1956. (1st edn., New York: Pantheon Books, 1949; Bollingen Series, 17.)

Eliade, Mircea, *Le mythe de l'éternel retour.* Paris: Gallimard, 1949. (Engl. trans. W. R. Trask, New York: Pantheon Books, 1954; Bollingen Series, 46.)

———, *Birth and Rebirth.* New York: Harper & Brothers, 1958a.

———, *Patterns in Comparative Religion.* New York: Sheed & Ward, 1958b.

Gayton, A. H., "The Orphic Myth in North America," *Journal of American Folklore,* 1935, *48:* 263-293.

Herskovits, M. J., and F. S. Herskovits, *Dahomean Narrative.* Evanston, Ill.: Northwestern University Press, 1958.

Ishida, Eiichiro, "The Mother-Son Complex in East Asiatic Religion and Folklore," in *Die Wiener Schule der Voelkerkunde, Festschrift zum 25 jährigen Bestand* (Vienna, 1955), pp. 411-419.

Jones, Ernest, *Hamlet and Oedipus,* New York: Doubleday Anchor Books, 1954. (Published first as an article in the *American Journal of Psychology* in 1910; again in 1923 as Ch. 1 in *Essays in Applied*

Psycho-Analysis; revised edn., London: V. Gollancz; New York: W. W. Norton, 1949.)

Kluckhohn, Clyde, "Myths and Rituals: A General Theory," *Harvard Theological Review,* 1942, *35:* 45-79.

Lessa, William, "Oedipus-Type Tales in Oceania," *Journal of American Folklore,* 1956, *69:* 63-73.

Lévi-Strauss, Claude, "The Structural Study of Myth," *Journal of American Folklore,* 1955, *68:* 428-445.

——, "Structure et dialectique," in Morris Halle (compiler), *For Roman Jakobson* (The Hague: Mouton, 1957), pp. 289-294.

Murdock, G. P., "World Ethnographic Sample," *American Anthropologist,* 1957, *59:* 664-688.

Raglan, Lord, *The Hero: A Study in Tradition, Myth and Drama.* New York: Vintage Books (Alfred A. Knopf), 1956. (1st edn., London: Methuen and Company, 1936.)

Rank, Otto, *The Myth of the Birth of the Hero,* trans. F. Robbins and S. E. Jellife. New York: Robert Brunner, 1952. (1st edn., *Der Mythus von der Geburt des Helden,* Leipzig-Wien: F. Deuticke, 1909.)

Róheim, Géza, *Psychoanalysis and Anthropology.* New York: International Universities Press, 1950.

Rooth, A. G., "The Creation Myths of the North American Indians," *Anthropos,* 1957, *52:* 497-508.

Spencer, Katherine, *Mythology and Value.* Memoir 48, American Folklore Society, Philadelphia, 1957.

SUGGESTIONS FOR DISCUSSION

1. What do Kluckhohn's conclusions suggest about the functions of myth?

2. What do Kluckhohn's findings on the universality of witchcraft myths suggest about the workings of the primitive mind?

3. Kluckhohn's treatment of Oedipal myths implies certain reservations about the psychoanalytical approach to myth. To what extent are these reservations shared by Dorson?

4. Kluckhohn finds appealing the view that mythology provides "a logical model capable of overcoming contradictions in a people's view of the world and what they have deduced from experience." How might Oedipal myths and hero myths, as he describes them, serve this purpose? How does this idea bear on Murray's discussion of the causes and effects of myths?

NEW DIRECTIONS FROM OLD

NORTHROP FRYE

In his essay on Edgar Allan Poe's *Eureka,* Paul Valéry speaks of cosmology as one of the oldest of literary arts. Not many people have clearly understood that cosmology is a literary form, not a religious or scientific one. It is true of course that religion and science have regularly been confused with, or more accurately confused by, cosmological structures. In the Middle Ages the Ptolemaic universe had close associations with contemporary theology and science as well as with poetry. But as science depends on experiment and religion on experience, neither is committed to a specific cosmology, or to any cosmology at all. Science blew up the Ptolemaic universe, and Christianity, after feeling itself cautiously all over, discovered that it had survived the explosion. The situation is very different in poetry. It is a gross error to study the cosmology of the *Commedia* or *Paradise Lost* as extraneous obsolete science, for the cosmology of these poems is not simply a part of their subject-matter, but inseparably a part of

NORTHROP FRYE, born at Sherbrooke, Quebec, in 1912, is professor of English and principal of Victoria College in the University of Toronto. He has also taught at Harvard, Princeton, Columbia, Indiana (School of Letters), Washington, and British Columbia for terms or summer sessions. His books include *Fearful Symmetry: A Study of William Blake;* and *Anatomy of Criticism;* and he has also written essays or chapters contributed to many other works.

their total form. Dante's love of symmetry, of which so many critics speak, is not a personal predilection, but an essential part of his poetic craftmanship.

Even in times when science gives little encouragement for it, poetry shows a tendency to return to the older cosmological structures, as Poe's *Eureka* itself shows. In chemistry the periodical table of elements may have replaced the old tetrad of fire, air, water and earth, but it is the traditional four that reappear in the Eliot Quartets. The universe of Dylan Thomas's "Altarwise by owl-light" sonnets is still geocentric and astrological; the structure of *Finnegans Wake* is held together by occult correspondence; no reputable scientist has had the influence on the poetry of the last century that Swedenborg or Blavatsky has had. Critics have often remarked on the archaic, even the atavistic, tendencies of poets, and nowhere are these tendencies better illustrated than in the reckless cosmological doodling that may be traced in poetry from Dante's *Convivio* to Yeats's *Vision*. A principle of some importance is involved here, nothing less in fact than the whole question of poetic thought, as distinct from other kinds of thought. Either Peacock's thesis is correct, that poets are a barbaric survival in a scientific age that has outgrown them, or there are requirements in poetic thinking that have never been carefully studied by critics. The graduate-school cliché that Dante's *Commedia* is the metaphysical system of St. Thomas translated into imagery is a melancholy example of how helpless criticism is to deal with one of its own subjects.

We are all familiar with the Aristotelian argument about the relation of poetry to action. Action, or *praxis,* is the world of events; and history, in the broadest sense, may be called a verbal imitation of action, or events put into the form of words. The historian imitates action directly: he makes specific statements about what happened, and is judged by the truth of what he says. What really happened is the external model of his pattern of words, and he is judged by the adequacy with which his words reproduce that model.

The poet, in dramas and epics at least, also imitates actions in words, like the historian. But the poet makes no specific statements of fact, and hence is not judged by the truth or falsehood of what he says. The poet has no external model for his imitation, and is judged by the integrity or consistency of his verbal structure. The reason is that he imitates the universal, not the particular; he is concerned not with what happened but with what happens. His subject-matter is the kind of thing that does happen, in other words the typical or recurring element in action. There is thus a close analogy between the poet's subject-matter and those significant actions that men engage in simply because they are typical and recurring, the actions that we call rituals. The verbal imitation of ritual is myth, and the typical action of poetry is the plot, or what Aristotle calls *mythos,* so that for the literary critic the Aristotelian term *mythos* and the English word myth are much the same thing. Such plots, because they describe typical actions, naturally fall into typical forms. One of these is the tragic plot, with its desis and lysis, its peripety and catastrophe, as charted in the *Poetics.* Another is the comic plot with its happy ending; another is the romance plot with its adventures and its final quest; another is the ironic plot, usually a parody of romance. The poet finds increasingly that he can deal with history only to the extent that history supplies him with, or affords a pretext for, the comic, tragic, romantic or ironic myths that he actually uses.

We notice that when a historian's scheme gets to a certain point of comprehensiveness it becomes mythical in shape, and so approaches the poetic in its structure. There are romantic historical myths based on a quest or pilgrimage to a City of God or a classless society; there are comic historical myths of progress through evolution or revolution; there are tragic myths of decline and fall, like the works of Gibbon and Spengler; there are ironic myths of recurrence or casual catastrophe. It is not necessary, of course, for such a myth to be a universal theory of history, but merely for it to be exemplified in whatever history is using it. A Canadian historian, F. H. Underhill, writing on Toynbee, has coined the term "metahistory" for such works. We notice that metahistory, though it usually tends to very long and erudite books, is far more popular than regular history: in fact metahistory is really the form in which most history reaches the general public. It is only the metahistorian, whether Spengler or Toynbee or H. G. Wells or a religious writer using history as his source of *exampla,* who has much chance of becoming a best-seller.

We notice also that the historian proper tends to confine his verbal imitations of action to human events. His instinct is to look always for the human cause; he avoids the miraculous or the providential; he may assess various non-human factors such as climate, but he keeps them in his "background." The poet, of course, is under no such limitation. Gods and ghosts may be quite as important characters for him as human beings; actions may be caused by *hybris* or nemesis, and the "pathetic fallacy" may be an essential part of his design. Here again metahistory resembles poetry. Metahistorical themes often assume an analogy, or even an identity, with natural processes. Spengler's *Decline of the West* is based on the analogy of historical cultures and vegetable life; Toynbee's "withdrawal and return" theme turns on the analogy of the natural cycle; most theories of progress during the last century have claimed some kind of kinship with evolution. All deterministic histories, whether the determining force is economics or geography or the providence of God, are based on an analogy between history and something else, and so are metahistorical.

The historian works inductively, collecting his facts and trying to avoid any informing patterns except those that he sees, or is honestly convinced he sees, in the facts themselves. The poet, like the metahistorian, works deductively. If he is going to write a tragedy, his decision to impose a tragic pattern on his subject is prior, in importance at least, to his decision to choose a specific historical or legendary or contemporary theme. The remark of Menander that so impressed Matthew Arnold, that his new play was finished and he had only to write it, is typical of the way the poet's mind works. No fact, however interesting, no image, however vivid, no phrase, however striking, no combination of sounds, however resonant, is of any use to a poet unless it fits: unless it appears to spring inevitably out of its context.

A historian in the position of Menander, ready to write his book, would say that he had finished his research and had only to put it into shape. He works toward his unifying form, as the poet works from it. The informing pattern of the

historian's book, which is his *mythos* or plot, is secondary,
just as detail to a poet is secondary. Hence the first thing that
strikes us about the relation of the poet to the historian is
their opposition. In a sense the historical is the opposite of
the mythical, and to tell a historian that what gives shape to
his book is a myth would sound to him vaguely insulting.
Most historians would prefer to believe, with Bacon, that
poetry is "feigned history," or, at least, that history is one
thing and poetry another, and that all metahistory is a bastard combination of two things that will not really combine.
But metahistory is too large and flourishing a growth to be
so easily weeded out, and such oversimplifying would elimi-
nate Tacitus and Thucydides equally with Buckle and Spengler. It would be better to recognize that metahistory has two
poles, one in history proper and the other in poetry. Historians, up to a point, know what the province of history is
and what its dependable methods are; but literary critics
know so little of the province or methods of either poetry or
criticism that it is natural for the historian to feel that one
pole of metahistory is real and the other imaginary, and that
whatever is poetic in a historical work destroys its value as
history. This is to assume that poetry is simply a form of per-
missible lying, but that is an assumption that critics have
never done much to refute.

Because of its concern with the universal rather than the
particular, poetry, Aristotle says, is more philosophical than
history. Aristotle never followed up this remark, to the extent
at least of working out the relation of poetry to conceptual
thought. Perhaps, however, we can reconstruct it along lines
similar to his discussion of the relation of poetry to action.
We may think, then, of literature as an area of verbal imitation midway between events and ideas, or, as Sir Philip Sidney
calls them, examples and precepts. Poetry faces, in one direction, the world of *praxis* or action, a world of events occurring
in time. In the opposite direction, it faces the world of
theoria, of images and ideas, the conceptual or visualizable
world spread out in space, or mental space. This world may
be imitated in a variety of ways, most commonly in words,
though composers, painters, mathematicians and others do
not think primarily in words. Still, there is a large area of

discursive writing, or works of science and philosophy, which makes up the primary verbal imitation of thought. The discursive writer puts ideas and images into words directly. Like the historian, he makes specific statements, or predications; and, like the historian, he is judged by the truth of what he says, or by the adequacy of his verbal reproduction of his external model.

The poet, similarly, is concerned, not with specific or particular predications, but with typical or recurring ones: "What oft was thought," in other words. The truism, the sententious axiom, the proverb, the *topos* or rhetorical commonplace, the irresistibly quotable phrase—such things are the very life-blood of poetry. The poet seeks the new expression, not the new content, and when we find profound or great thoughts in poetry we are usually finding a statement of a common human situation wittily or inevitably expressed. "The course of true love never did run smooth" is from a Shakespearean comedy, and such sententious comments have been a conventional feature of comedy at least since Menander, whose stock of them was raided by St. Paul. The pleasure we get from quoting such axioms is derived from the versatility with which they fit a great variety of situations with an unexpected appositeness. There are serious works on theology and economics that use a quotation from *Alice in Wonderland* as a motto for each chapter.

Again, the poet has more in common with the constructive elements in thought, and less in common with its descriptive elements. Versified science, whether obsolete or up to date, as we have it in various encyclopedic poems from medieval times onward, never seems able to get beyond a certain point of poetic merit. It is not that the poets are unskillful, but that there is something wrong with the organizing form of the poem. The unifying theme of the *Ormulum* or *The Pastime of Pleasure* is not itself poetic in outline. We may compare the versified historical chronicles of Robert of Gloucester or William Warner, in which we also retain only a languid literary interest, and for the same reason. Poetry seems to have a good deal more affinity with speculative systems, which from Lucretius to *The Testament of Beauty* have consistently shown a more poetic shape. It looks as though there were something of the same kind of affinity between poetry and metaphysics that there is between poetry and metahistory. Of late years we have become much more impressed with the element of *construct* in metaphysical systems, with the feature in them that seems most closely to resemble the poetic. There are logicians who regard metaphysics as bastard logic, just as there are historians who regard metahistory as bastard history. Everything is most properly symmetrical.

The only defect in the symmetry is that metaphysics seems to work mainly with abstractions, and poetry has a limited tolerance for abstractions. Poetry is, in Milton's words, more simple, sensuous and passionate than philosophy. Poetry seeks the image rather than the idea, and even when it deals with ideas it tends to seek the latent basis of concrete imagery in the idea. A discursive nineteenth-century writer will talk of progress and advance in history without noticing, or deliberately ignoring, the fact that his idea has been suggested by the invention of the railway. Tennyson will say "Let the great world spin for ever down the ringing grooves of change," getting his mechanical facts wrong, as poets will, but hitting his conceptual target straight in its sensational bullseye. Literary criticism finds a good deal of difficulty in dealing with such works as *Sartor Resartus,* which appear to employ philosophical concepts and seem to be stating propositions, and yet are clearly something else than actual philosophy. *Sartor Resartus* takes the structure of German Romantic philosophy and extracts from it a central metaphor in which the phenomenal is to the noumenal world as clothing is to the naked body: something which conceals it, and yet, by enabling it to appear in public, paradoxically reveals it as well.

The "ideas" the poets use, therefore, are not actual propositions, but thought-forms or conceptual myths, usually dealing with images rather than abstractions, and hence normally unified by metaphor, or image-phrasing, rather than by logic. The mechanical or diagrammatic image referred to above is a clear example of the poetic element in thought. We sometimes get explicit diagrams in philosophical thought, such as Plato's divided line and Aristotle's middle way, but the great chain of being is more typically a poetic conceptual myth, because it is a device for classifying images. The chain is only one of a great variety of mechanical models in poetic thought, some of them preceding by centuries the machines that embody them. There are the wheels of fate and fortune, mirrors (the word "reflection" indicates how deeply rooted the conceptual world is in the mechanism of the eye), internal combustion or vital spark metaphors, the geared machinery of so much nineteenth-century scientism, the thermostat and feedback metaphors which, since at least Burke's time and certainly long before "cybernetics," have organized most democratic political thought.

Just as we are initially aware of an opposition between the historical and the mythical, so we are initially aware of an opposition between the scientific and the systematic. The scientist starts out empirically, and tries to avoid hampering himself with such gigantic constructs as "universe" or "substance." Similarly, the idea "God," taken as a scientific hypothesis, has never been anything but a nuisance to science. God himself, in the Book of Job, is represented as warning man of this when he points out to Job that the conception "creation," as an objective fact, is not and never can be contained by human experience. Such constructive concepts are at least metaphysical, and metaphysics, as its etymology indicates, comes after physical science. In theology the deductive tendency has completely taken over, as there can hardly be such a thing as empirical theology. The next step brings us to poetic mythology, the concrete, sensational, figurative, anthropomorphic basis out of which the informing concepts of discursive thought come.

II

In its use of images and symbols, as in its use of ideas, poetry seeks the typical and recurring. That is one reason why throughout the history of poetry the basis for organizing the imagery of the physical world has been the natural cycle. The sequence of seasons, times of day, periods of life and death, have helped to provide for literature the combination of movement and order, of change and regularity, that is needed in all the arts. Hence the importance, in poetic symbolism, of the mythical figure known as the dying god, whether Adonis or

Proserpine or their innumerable allotropic forms, who represents the cycle of nature.

Again, for poets, the physical world has usually been not only a cyclical world but a "middle earth," situated between an upper and a lower world. These two worlds reflect in their form the heavens and hells of the religions contemporary with the poet, and are normally thought of as abodes of unchanging being, not as cyclical. The upper world is reached by some form of ascent, and is a world of gods or happy souls. The most frequent images of ascent are the mountain, the tower, the winding staircase or ladder, or a tree of cosmological dimensions. The upper world is often symbolized by the heavenly bodies, of which the one nearest us is the moon. The lower world, reached by descent through a cave or under water, is more oracular and sinister, and as a rule is or includes a place of torment and punishment. It follows that there would be two points of particular significance in poetic symbolism. One is the point, usually the top of a mountain just below the moon, where the upper world and this one come into alignment, where we look up to the heavenly world and down on the turning cycle of nature. The other is the point, usually in a mysterious labyrinthine cave, where the lower world and this one come into alignment, where we look down to a world of pain and up to the turning cycle of nature. This upward perspective sees the same world, though from the opposite pole, as the downward perspective in the vision of ascent, and hence the same cyclical symbols may be employed for it.

The definitive literary example of the journey of ascent is in the last half-dozen cantos of Dante's *Purgatorio*. Here Dante, climbing a mountain in the form of a winding stair, purges himself of his last sin at the end of Canto 26, and then finds that he has recovered his lost youth, not his individual but his generic youth as a child of Adam, and hence is in the garden of Eden, the Golden Age of Classical mythology, a lower Paradise directly below the moon, where Paradise proper begins. This point is as far up as Virgil can go, and after Virgil leaves Dante the great apocalyptic vision of the Word and the Church begins. We are told in Canto 28 that Eden is a *locus amoenus,* a place of perpetually temperate climate, from which the seeds of vegetable life in the world below proceed, and to which they return—in other words Eden is at the apex of the natural cycle. In Eden Dante sees the maiden Matilda, who, he says in the same canto, makes him remember where and what Proserpine was, when her mother lost her and she lost the spring flowers. Earlier, in Canto 27, the dying god's conventional emblem, the red or purple flower, is dropped into the imagery with a reference to Pyramus and Thisbe. As a garden is a place of trees, the tree itself is, like the mountain-top, a natural symbol of the vision of ascent, and enters Dante's vision, first in Canto 29 in the form of the seven candlesticks, which look like golden trees at a distance, and later in Canto 32 as the tree of knowledge, which turns purple in color.

The Gardens of Adonis episode in Book Three of *The Faerie Queene* is a familiar English example of *locus amoenus* symbolism. The Gardens of Adonis are spoken of as a "Paradise," and are, again, a place of seed from which the forms of life in the cycle of nature proceed, and to which they return. In Spenser we have the dying god Adonis, the purple flower amaranthus (associated with Sidney, whose fatal thigh-wound made him a favorite historical embodiment of Adonis) and a grove of myrtle trees on top of a mountain. One of Spenser's earliest and acutest critics, Henry Reynolds, suggests, in the easy-going fashion of his time, an etymological connection between Adonis and Eden, but Spenser does not make any explicit link between this garden and Eden, which is the kingdom of Una's parents in Book One. Nor does he explicitly locate the Gardens at the apex of the cyclical world just below the moon, though he does speak of Adonis as "eterne in mutabilitie," which reminds us of the *Mutabilitie Cantoes* and of the dispute between Mutability and Jove, held in the sphere of the moon at the boundary of Jove's world. In this poem the evidence brought forward by Mutability in her favor, which consists of various aspects of the natural cycle, proves Jove's case instead, because it is evidence of a principle of stability in flux. In any case the upper location of the Gardens of Adonis seems to be in Milton's mind when in *Comus* he introduces the Attendant Spirit as coming from the Gardens of Adonis, which according to the opening

line are "Before the starry threshold of Jove's Court." Milton
also places Eden on a mountain-top, protected by a "verdur-
ous wall," and the world into which Adam is exiled is spoken
of as a "subjected plain."

In Biblical typology the relation between Eden and the
wilderness of Adam's exile is closely parallel to the relation
between the Promised Land and the wilderness of the law.
Here again the Promised Land is thought of as being "above"
the wilderness, its capital being Jerusalem, the center of the
world and the city on the mountain, "whither the tribes go
up." The same kind of language enters the prophetic visions:
Ezekiel's wilderness vision of dry bones is in a valley, while
the panorama of the restored Jerusalem with which the
prophecy concludes begins with the prophet seated "upon a
very high mountain." In *Paradise Regained* Christ's temptation in the wilderness is really a descent into hell, or the domain of Satan, terminated by his successful stand on the
pinnacle of Jerusalem, which prefigures his later conquest of
the lower world of death and hell, much as Satan prefigures
his own success in Eden when he sits "like a cormorant," in
the tree of life, the highest point in the garden. Christ's victory over Satan also, Milton says, "raised" Eden in the wilderness. The forty days of the temptation are commemorated in
Lent, which is immediately followed in the calendar by
Easter; they also correspond to the forty years of wilderness
wandering under the law, which was terminated by the conquest of the Promised Land by Joshua, who has the same
name as Jesus (cf. *Paradise Lost* xii, 307-314).

T. S. Eliot's *Ash Wednesday* is a poem founded on Dante's
Purgatorio which at the same time glances at these Biblical
and liturgical typologies. The central image of the poem is
the winding stair of Dante's mountain, which leads to a
Paradisal garden. Overtones of Israel in the wilderness ("This
is the land. We have our inheritance."), of Ezekiel's valley of
dry bones, and of course of Lent, are also present. As the poet
is preoccupied with ascent, we get only fitful glimpses of the
natural cycle on the way up: "a slotted window bellied like
the fig's fruit," "hawthorn blossom," and a "broadbacked
figure drest in blue and green," the last reappearing in a subdued form as a silent "garden god" in the *locus amoenus*

above. In the final section the poet returns from the universal past to the individual past, from "the violet and the violet" of the garden to a nostalgia symbolized among other things by "lost lilacs."

In view of the explicit and avowed debt of this poem to the *Purgatorio,* the parallels in imagery may not seem very significant. It is all the more interesting to compare the treatment of the "winding stair" image in Yeats, as there, whatever influence from Dante there may be, the attitude taken towards the ascent is radically different. Two of Yeats's poems, *A Dialogue of Self and Soul* and *Vacillation,* turn on a debate between a "soul" who wants only to ascend the stair to some ineffable communion beyond, and a "self" or "heart" who is fascinated by the downward vision into nature, even to the point of accepting rebirth in its cycle. In the former poem the "self" focuses its gaze on the dying-god symbol of the Japanese ceremonial sword wrapped in silk embroidered with flowers of "heart's purple." In *Vacillation* the symbol of ascent and separation from the cycle, the uncorrupted body of the saint, is contrasted with the cycle itself of death and corruption and rebirth, represented by the lion and honeycomb of Samson's riddle. Here, however, it is the symbol of the tree, associated with "Attis' image" and, somewhat like Dante's candlestick vision, "half all glittering flame and half all green," that dominates the poem, and that seems to combine in itself the images of ascent and cycle. Similarly in *Among School Children* the contrast between the nun and the mother, the "bronze repose" of direct ascent and the cyclical "honey of generation," is resolved in the image of the chestnut tree.

There are other examples of the green world at the top of the natural cycle in modern poetry. Wallace Stevens, for instance, gives us a very clear description of it in *Credences of Summer*:

> It is the natural tower of all the world,
> The point of survey, green's green apogee,
> But a tower more precious than the view beyond,
> A point of survey squatting like a throne,
> Axis of everything.

But in the twentieth century, on the whole, images of descent are, so to speak, in the ascendant. These derive mainly from the sixth book of the Aeneid, and its progenitor in the eleventh book of the Odyssey. Here also one is confronted with two levels, a lower world of unending pain, the world of Tantalus and Sisyphus and Ixion, and an upper world more closely connected with the natural cycle. In Virgil there is a most elaborate development of cyclical and rebirth symbolism, introducing speculations of a type that are rarely encountered again in Western poetry before at least Romantic times. In the vision of descent, where we enter a world of darkness and mystery, there is more emphasis on initiation, on learning the proper rites, on acquiring effective talismans like the golden bough. The main figures have a strongly parental aura about them: in Virgil the prophet of the future of Rome is Aeneas' father, and the maternal figure is represented by the Sibyl. In Homer, Odysseus' mother appears, and the figure corresponding to Virgil's Sibyl is Circe, whom Homer calls *potnia,* which means something like reverend. At the top of the winding stair one normally attains direct knowledge or vision, but the reward of descent is usually oracular or esoteric knowledge, concealed or forbidden to most people, often the knowledge of the future.

In romance, where descent themes are very common, the hero often has to kill or pacify a dragon who guards a secret hoard of wealth or wisdom. The descent is also often portrayed as a mimic, temporary or actual death of the hero; or he may be swallowed by the dragon, so that his descent is into the monster's belly. In medieval treatments of the Christian story some of these themes reappear. Between his death on the cross and his resurrection Jesus descends into hell, often portrayed, especially in fresco, as the body of a huge dragon or shark, which he enters by the mouth, like his prototype Jonah. Again there are two levels in the lower world: hell proper, a world of endless torment, and the upper limbo which is "harrowed," and from which the redeemed, among whom the parental figures Adam and Eve have an honored place, return to the upper world. The monster's open mouth recurs in *Ash Wednesday* as "the toothed gullet of an agèd shark," and as the symbol of the "blue rocks" or Symplegades, whose clashing together has similar overtones.

For obvious reasons, visions of descent in medieval and Renaissance poetry are usually infernal visions, based on Virgil but ignoring his interest in rebirth. Only with Romantic poetry do we begin to get once more the oracular or quest descent, where the hero gets something more from his descent than a tragic tale or an inspection of torments. In Keats's *Endymion* there are adventures in both upward and downward directions, the upward ones being mainly quests for beauty and the downward ones quests for truth. The Gardens of Adonis in this poem seem to be down rather than up, as they do at the conclusion of Blake's *Book of Thel,* though in that conclusion there is a sudden reversal of perspective. Shelley's *Prometheus Unbound* is a more striking example of a cosmology in which everything beneficial comes from below, and everything sinister from above. The contrast here with the cosmology of Dante and Milton is so striking that it deserves more examination.

In Dante, in Spenser, in Milton, the foreground of symbols and images seems to be portrayed against a background of roughly four levels of existence. I need a word for this background, and am strongly tempted to steal "topocosm" from Theodor H. Gaster's *Thespis,* though he uses it in a quite different sense. The top level is the place of the presence of God, the empyreal heaven, which operates in this world as the order of grace and providence. The next level is that of human nature properly speaking, represented by the garden of Eden or the Golden Age before the Fall, and now a world to be regained internally by moral and intellectual effort. Third is the level of physical nature, morally neutral but theologically fallen, which man is born into but can never adjust to, and fourth is the level of sin, death and corruption, which since the Fall has permeated the third level too. Throughout this period it was traditional to symbolize the top level by the starry spheres, the spiritual by the physical heaven. Dante's upper Paradise is located in the planetary spheres, and in Milton's *Nativity Ode* the music of the spheres, symbol of the understanding of unfallen man, is in counterpoint to the chorus of descending angels.

After the rise of Copernican astronomy and Newtonian physics, the starry sky becomes a less natural and a more perfunctory and literary metaphor for the spiritual world. The stars look increasingly less like vehicles of angelic intelligences, and come to suggest rather a mechanical and mindless revolution. This shift of perspective is of course already present in a famous passage in Pascal, but it does not make its full impact on poetry until much later. A deity at home in such a world would seem stupid or malignant, at best a kind of self-hypnotized Pangloss. Hence the variety of stupid sky-gods in Romantic poetry: Blake's Urizen, Shelley's Jupiter, Byron's Arimanes, Hardy's Immanent Will, perhaps the God of the Prologue to *Faust*. Blake, the closest of this group to the orthodox Christian tradition, points out that there is more Scriptural evidence for Satan as a sky god than for Jesus. Even more significant for poetic symbolism is the sense of the mechanical complications of starry movement as the projection or reflection of something mechanical and malignant in human nature. In other words, the Frankenstein theme of actualizing human death-impulses in some form of fateful mechanism has a strong natural connection with the sky or "outer space," and in modern science fiction is reguarly attached to it. At the same time poets in the Romantic period tend to think of nature less as a structure or system, set over against the conscious mind as an object, and more as a body of organisms from which the human organism proceeds, nature being the underlying source of humanity, as the seed is of the plant.

Hence with Romanticism another "topocosm," almost the reverse of the traditional one, begins to take shape. On top is the bleak and frightening world of outer space. Next comes the level of ordinary human experience, with all its anomalies and injustices. Below, in the only place left for any *locus amoenus,* is the buried original form of society, now concealed under the historical layers of civilization. With a modern Christian poet this would be the old unfallen world, or its equivalent: thus in Auden's *For the Time Being* the "garden" world is hidden within or concealed by the "wilderness" of ordinary life. With a poet closer to Rousseau this buried society would be the primitive society of nature and reason,

the sleeping beauty that a revolutionary act of sufficient courage would awaken. On the fourth level, corresponding to the
traditional hell or world of death, is the mysterious reservoir
of power and life out of which both nature and humanity
proceed. This world is morally ambivalent, being too archaic
for distinctions of good and evil, and so retains some of the
sinister qualities of its predecessor. Hence the insistence in
Romantic culture of the ambivalent nature of "genius," or
an unusual degree of natural creative power, which may destroy the poet's personality or drive him to various forms of
evil or suffering, as in the Byronic hero, the *poète maudit,* the
compulsive sinner of contemporary Christian and existential
fiction, and other varieties of Romantic agony.

Against this "topocosm" the action of *Prometheus Unbound* seems logical enough. In the sky is Jupiter, the projection of human superstition with its tendency to deify a
mechanical and sub-human order. Below is the martyred
Prometheus; below him Mother Earth (in whose domain is
included the world of death, which has a mysterious but recurring connection with the *locus amoenus* in Shelley), and
at the bottom of the whole action is the oracular cave of
Demogorgon, who calls himself Eternity, and from whom the
power proceeds that rejuvenates Earth, liberates Prometheus,
and annihilates Jupiter. (On the mythical structure of *Prometheus Unbound* see, now, Harold Bloom, *Shelley's Mythmaking,* a study not available to me when writing this essay.)

The Romantic "topocosm," like its predecessor, is, for the
poet, simply a way of arranging metaphors, and does not in
itself imply any particular attitudes or beliefs or conceptions.
The traditional infernal journey naturally persists: Eliot's
Waste Land and the first of Pound's *Cantos* are closely related
examples, the former having many Aeneid echoes and the
latter being based on the Odyssey. In Pound the characteristic
parental figure is Aphrodite, called "venerendam," an echo
of Homer's *potnia,* who bears the "golden bough of Argi-
cida," in other words of Hermes the psychopomp. In Eliot
the parallel figure to this combination of Hermes and Aphrodite is the hermaphroditic Teiresias, the seer who was the
object of Odysseus' descent.

The "topocosm" of Dante was closely related to contemporary religious and scientific constructs, and to a much lesser degree the same is true of the post-Romantic one. We get our "up" metaphors from the traditional forms: everything that is uplifting or aspiring about the spiritual quest, such as the wings of angels or the ascension of Christ or the phrase "lift up your hearts," is derived from the metaphorical association of God and the sky. Even as late as the nineteenth century, progress and evolution were still going up as well as on. In the last century or so there has been a considerable increase in the use of approving "down" metaphors: to get "down" to bedrock or brass tacks or the basic facts is now the sign of a proper empirical procedure. Descent myths are also deeply involved in the social sciences, especially psychology, where we have a subconscious or unconscious mind assumed, by a spatial metaphor, to be underneath the consciousness, and into this mind we descend in quest of parental figures. The Virgilian inspiration of modern scientific mythology is not hard to see: the golden bough of the sixth book of the Aeneid supplies the title and theme for Frazer, and the famous line spoken by Juno in the seventh, that if she cannot prevail on the high gods she will stir up hell (fletere si nequeo superos, Acheronta movebo), is the apt motto of Freud's *Interpretation of Dreams*. But now that politics and science at least are beginning to focus once more on the moon, it is possible that a new construct will be formed, and a new table of metaphors organize the imagery of our poets.

SUGGESTIONS FOR DISCUSSION

1. How is it, according to Frye, that cosmological systems are more in the province of poetry than in that of science?
2. How does Frye distinguish poetic thought from historical thought? By what standards would he have poetry judged, if not by the standard of truth? How close is Frye's position on this matter to Murray's position on the "truth" of myths?
3. Given Frye's view of poetry, why is it the natural home of myth? Why does a preoccupation with universals (rather than particulars) lead poets away from science and history and toward myth?
4. What seems to explain the attractiveness, to poets, of the imagery of upper world and lower world? What psychic function might this cosmology serve?
5. Frye outlines two "topocosms," that of the Christian humanists and that of the romantics, and he hints at the possibility that a new one

is in the process of formation. What traces do you see around you of such a "new table of metaphors"? Can you think of other "topocosms" that have appealed to at least some modern writers? To political thinkers? To the creators of television and cinema art?

THE YEARNING FOR PARADISE

IN PRIMITIVE TRADITION

MIRCEA ELIADE

In his book on the myths of the African peoples Hermann Baumann sums up the myths of a primeval paradisial era. In those times, he says, men did not know of death: they understood the language of the animals and were at peace with them; they did not work, and found abundant nourishment at hands' reach. Following upon a certain mythical event —which we will not undertake to discuss—this paradisial stage ended and humanity became what we know it to be today.[1]

We encounter the "paradise myth" all over the world in more or less complex forms. Besides the paramount paradisial

MIRCEA ELIADE was born in Bucharest in 1907. After acquiring his degree in literature, he studied philosophy at the University of Calcutta (1928-1932). His doctoral dissertation, *Yoga: Essai sur les Origines de la Mystique Indienne,* was published in Paris and Bucharest in 1936. He has taught at the Universities of Bucharest, Rome, Marburg, Munich, Uppsala, and Lund, at the Ecole des Hautes Etudes of the Sorbonne, at the Istituto Italiano per l'Estremo Oriente, and at the Jung Institute at Zurich. Since 1957 he has been professor of the history of religion at the University of Chicago. His publications include: *The Myth of the Eternal Return; Patterns in Comparative Religion; Birth and Rebirth; Yoga: Immortality and Freedom; The Sacred and the Profane; Le Chamanisme; Images et Symboles; Forgerons et Alchimistes;* and *Mythes, Rêves et Mystères.*

note, it always has a certain number of characteristic elements, chiefly the idea of immortality. These myths may be classified into two great categories: first, those concerning the primordial close proximity between Heaven and Earth; and second, those refering to an actual means of communication between Heaven and Earth. This is not the place to analyze the many variations of each of these two types, nor to give precise indications of the areas of their distribution or their chronology. For our purposes, a single feature concerns us: in describing the primordial situation the myths reveal its paradisial quality by the fact that *in illo tempore* Heaven is said to have been very near Earth, or that it was easy to reach it by means of a tree, a vine, or a ladder, or by climbing a mountain. When Heaven was rudely "separated" from Earth, when it became "distant" as it is today, when the tree or the vine leading from Earth to Heaven was cut, or the mountain which touched Heaven was leveled—the paradisial state was over and humanity arrived at its present state.

Actually, all these myths show primitive man enjoying blessedness, spontaneity, and liberty, which he has most annoyingly lost as the consequence of the "fall," that is, as the result of a mythical occurrence which has brought about the rupture between Heaven and Earth. *In illo tempore,* in that paradisial time, the gods descended to Earth and mingled with men, and men could ascend to Heaven by climbing a mountain, a tree, a vine, or a ladder, or have themselves carried there by the birds.

A careful ethnological analysis will throw light on the cultural context of each of these two types of myths. For example, it may be possible to show that the myths about the extreme nearness of Heaven and Earth are found primarily in Oceania and in southeast Asia and are in some way connected with a matriarchal ideology.[2] And again, it might show that the mythical symbol of an *Axis mundi*—mountain, tree, vine, which occupies the "center of the Earth" and connects Earth with Heaven, a symbol already found among the most primitive tribes (Australia, pigmies, Arctic regions, etc.) —has been developed principally in pastoral and sedentary cultures, and has been handed on to the great urban cultures of Eastern antiquity.[3] But we need not go into these ethnological analyses. For the purposes of this article the classification of the myths will suffice.

Let us enumerate the specific characteristics of the man of the "paradisial" period without considering their respective contexts: immortality, spontaneity, liberty, the ability to ascend to Heaven and "easy access" to the gods, friendship with the animals and knowledge of their language. This combination of privileges and powers was lost in consequence of a primordial event: the "fall" of man may be interpreted equally well by an ontological mutation in his own state as by a cosmic rupture.

It is, however, not uninteresting to find that through the exercise of special techniques the shaman tries to overcome the actual conditions of human life—those affecting "fallen man"—and to reconstitute the state of primordial man as we know it by the "paradisial myths." We know that among the other manipulators of religion in archaic cultures the shaman is the specialist in ecstasy *par excellence*. It is because of his ecstatic power—thanks to the fact that he can at will leave his material body and undertake mystical journeys anywhere in the cosmos—that the shaman can be healer and guide as well as mystic and visionary. None but the shaman can follow the wandering and lost soul of the diseased, capture and restore it to its body. It is he who accompanies the souls of the dead to their new dwellings. No other than he may undertake the long ecstatic journeys to Heaven to lay before the gods the soul of the sacrificed animal and pray for the divine blessing. In a word, the shaman is the expert in "matters of the spirit"; he, above all others, knows the various dramas, risks, and perils that concern "the soul." For "primitive" societies, the whole complex "shaman" represents what, in more elaborated religions, we have agreed to call mysticism and mystical experience.

The shamanic séance usually contains the following elements: (1) call of the auxiliary spirits (for the most part these are animals) and conversation with them in a secret language; (2) drum playing and dancing in preparation for the mystic journey; (3) the trance (feigned or real) during which the soul of the shaman is considered to have left his body. The goal of the whole shamanic séance is to arrive at ecstasy, for only in ecstasy can the shaman "fly" through the air, or "descend into Hell," in other words, fulfill his mission of healer and psychic guide.

It is significant that in order to prepare for the trance the shaman makes use of a "secret language," or, as it is called in some regions, "the language of animals." On the one hand, the shaman imitates the behavior of the animals; on the other, he tries to imitate their cries, above all, those of birds. Shiero-szewski has observed it among the Yakutsk shamans: [4]

Mysterious noises are audible sometimes from above, some-times from below, sometimes in front of, sometimes behind the shaman. . . . You seem to hear the plaintive call of the lapwing mingled with the croaking of a falcon interrupted by the whistle of the woodcock—all that is the voice of the shaman, varying the intonations of his voice—you hear the screaming of eagles min-gled with the plaints of the lapwing, the sharp tones of the wood-cock and the refrain of the cuckoo.

Castagné describes the *baqça* of the Kirghiz-Tatars, "Imi-tating with remarkable fidelity the songs of the birds and the sound of their wings." [5] As Lehtisalo has observed, a good share of the words used by the shaman during the séance have their origin in the cries of birds and other animals. This is particularly true with regard to the refrains and the yodeling, most frequently founded on onomatopeia, on phonemes and trills which plainly show that they come from the calls as well as the songs of birds.[6] In general, the shaman speaks during the séance with a high voice, a head tone, a falsetto, as if to emphasize that it is not he who speaks but a "spirit" or a "god." But we must note at this point that the same high voice is used as a rule for intoning magic formulas. "Magic" and "song"—especially song like birdsong—are often desig-nated by the same word. The Germanic term for the magic formula is *galdr* used with the verb *galan*, "to sing," which is applied more particularly to the cries of birds.

If one takes into account the fact that during his initiation the shaman is supposed to meet an animal who will reveal to him certain secrets of his profession, teach him "the language of animals," or become his "helper-spirit" (familiar) it is easier to understand the relations of friendship and familiarity which are established between the shaman and the animals: he speaks their language and becomes their friend and their master. We must say at once that to obtain the friendship of the animals so that they freely accept his control over them does not, to the mind of the primitive, imply any regression on the part of the shaman to a lower biological rank or stage. In one respect the animals are the bearers of a symbolism and mythology very significant for the religious life; to have contact with them, to speak their language, to become their friend and master means the possession of a spiritual life much more abundant than the simple human life of an ordinary mortal. In another sense, and as viewed by primitive man, animals possess considerable prestige, inasmuch as they know the secrets of life and of nature and even possess the secrets of longevity and immortality. Thus, in returning to the condition of the animals, the shaman comes to share their secret knowledge and enjoys the fuller life which is theirs.

We should emphasize this fact: friendship with the animals and knowledge of their language represents a "paradisial" syndrome. *In illo tempore,* before the "fall," such friendship was an integral part of the primordial situation. The shaman restores part of the "paradisial" situation of primordial man and he does this by recovering animal spontaneity (imitating animal behavior) and speaking animal language (imitation of animal sounds). It is important to state that the dialogue with the animals or their "incorporation" by the shaman (a mystic phenomenon not to be confused with "possession") constitutes the pre-ecstatic stage of the séance. The shaman cannot abandon his body and set out on his mystic journey before he has recovered, by his intimacy with the animals, a blessedness and a spontaneity inaccessible to his profane, everyday state. The vital experience of this friendship with the animals advances him far beyond the general situation of "fallen" humanity, while it permits him to return to *illud tempus* of the "paradisial" myths.

As for the state of ecstasy itself, it comprises, as we have seen, the abandonment of the body and the mystical journey to Heaven or to Hell. Here one fact is of supreme interest: namely, that the shaman's ascent to heaven is accomplished by the instrumentality of a tree or upright pole, symbols of the Cosmic Tree or Pole. Thus the Altaic shaman uses for the séance a young birch tree with its lower branches lopped and seven, nine, or twelve steps cut into the trunk. The tree symbolizes the Tree of the World, the seven, nine, or twelve steps represent the seven, nine or twelve Heavens, in other words, the different celestial levels. After having sacrificed a horse, the shaman climbs the steps, one after the other, till he reaches the ninth Heaven where Bai Ulgan, the supreme God, resides. As he ascends he describes to his audience, in great detail, everything he sees in each one of the Heavens. Finally, in the ninth Heaven he falls down before Bai Ulgan and offers him the soul of the sacrificial horse. This episode is the climax of the ecstatic ascent of the shaman: he collapses exhausted. After some time, he rubs his eyes, as though waking from deep sleep and greets the audience as though returning after long absence.[7]

The symbolism of the heavenly ascension by means of a tree is also clearly exemplified by the initiation ceremony of the Buriat shamans. The candidate clambers up a birch tree inside the hut, reaches the top and exits through the vent made for the smoke. But this vent for the smoke is known to represent the "hole" made by the polar star in the firmament. (Among other races the tent pole is called "Pole of the World" and likened to the polar star which also holds the tent of heaven like a pole and is called "Nail of Heaven.") Thus the ceremonial birch inside the hut is a representation of the "Cosmic Tree" which is located in the "Center of the World" and at the top of which shines the polar star. By climbing it, the candidate enters Heaven, and that is why, when he has left the tent by the vent, he shouts to invoke the help of the gods; up there he is in their presence.[8]

A similar symbolism explains the role of the shamanic drum. Emsheimer has shown that the dreams or initiation ecstasies of the future shamans signify a mystic journey on the Cosmic Tree at whose summit resides the Lord of the World. From one of the branches of that tree, dropped by the Lord for that purpose, the shaman fashions the cylinder of his drum.[9] We know that the Cosmic Tree is supposed to be at the "Center of the World" and that it connects Heaven and Earth. Because the cylinder of the drum comes from the very wood of the Cosmic Tree, the shaman, while drumming, is magically brought close to that tree, that is, to the Center of the World, where there is a possibility of going from one cosmic level to another.

Accordingly, whether he climbs the seven or nine steps cut into the ceremonial birch tree, or whether he beats his drum, the shaman is on his way to Heaven. In the first case, he laboriously mimics the ascent of the Cosmic Tree; in the second, he "flies" to the tree by the magic action of his drum. "Shamanic flight" is in any case very frequent and often identified with the ecstasy itself. Among the numerous variations of "shamanic flight" we are chiefly interested in the "flight" to the "Center of the World"; there we find the Tree, the Mountain, the Cosmic Pole, which connect Earth with Heaven. And it is there that we find the "hole" made by the polar star. As he climbs the Mountain, as he ascends the Tree, as he flies or comes up through the "hole" to the summit of the heavenly vault, the shaman effects his ascent to Heaven.

We know that *in illo tempore,* in the mythical time of "Paradise," there was a Mountain, a Tree, a Pole, or a Vine which connected Earth with Heaven and that primorial man could readily pass from one to the other by climbing them. Communication with Heaven was easy *in illo tempore,* and the meeting with the gods took place in actuality. The memory of these "paradisial" days is still very lively among "primitive" people. The Koryaks remember the mythical era of the hero Great Crow when men could ascend to Heaven without trouble; they add that in our days only the shamans can do this. The Bakairi of Brazil believe that for the shaman Heaven is no higher than a house, and therefore he can reach it in the twinkling of an eye.[10]

This means that during this ecstasy the shaman recovers the "paradisial" state. He re-establishes the easy communications as *in illo tempore* between Heaven and Earth. For him the Mountain or the Cosmic Tree again becomes the actual method of attaining Heaven, such as it was before the "fall." For the shaman, Heaven again comes close to Earth; no higher than a house, just as it was before the primordial rupture. Furthermore, the shaman re-establishes friendly relations with the animals. In other words, the ecstasy restores,

though only provisionally and for a restricted number of persons—the "mystics"—the initial state of all humanity. Thus
the mystic experience of "primitive" peoples is equivalent to
a *return to the beginning,* a reversion to the mythical days
of a "Lost Paradise." For the shaman in the state of ecstasy,
this world, this fallen world—which according to modern
terminology is governed by the laws of Time and History—
no longer exists. True, there is a great difference between the
situation of primordial man and that restored by the shaman
during ecstasy; the shaman can only temporarily abolish the
rupture between Heaven and Earth. He ascends to Heaven
"in spirit," no longer *in concreto* as did primordial man. He
does not abrogate death (all the ideas of immortality found
among primitive peoples imply—as they do among civilized
ones—a preliminary death; that is to say, that the immortality
is always a post-mortem, "spiritual" one).

To sum up: the paramount mystic experience of primitive
societies, that is to say, shamanism, reveals this "yearning for
Paradise," the wish to return to a state of blessedness and
liberty such as existed before the "fall," to restore contact
between Heaven and Earth; in a word, it reveals the wish to
abolish everything which has changed in the structure of the
Cosmos itself and in the manner of man's existence since the
primordial break. The ecstasy of the shaman recovers largely
the paradisial situation: he has regained the friendship of the
animals; by his "flight" or by his ascension he has again linked
Heaven and Earth; up there in Heaven he meets again face
to face the celestial Being and speaks to him in person as he
was wont to do *in illo tempore.*

One finds an analogous situation in the most recent and
most elaborate mysticism in existence, namely in Christian
mysticism. Christianity is dominated by the yearning for
Paradise. Turning to the East during prayer is connected
with paradisial themes—it appears as an expression of the
yearning for Paradise.[11] The same symbolism of paradise is
attested in the ritual of baptism: "Contrasted with Adam,
who falls under the domination of Satan and is driven from
Paradise, the catechumen is as though freed from such domination by the New Adam and led back to Paradise." [12]

Christianity thus appears as the realization of Paradise. "Christ is the Tree of Life" (Ambrosius, *De Isaac*, 5, 43) or the "fount of Paradise" (Ambrosius, *De Paradiso*, 3, 272, 10). But this realization of Paradise is on three successive levels. Baptism is the entrance into Paradise (Cyril of Jerusalem, *Procatech*. P. G. xxxiii, 357A); the life of mysticism is a deeper penetration into Paradise (Ambrosius, *De Paradiso*, I, I); finally death conducts the martyrs into Paradise (*Passio Perpet.*, P.L. III, 28a). It is indeed remarkable that we find this paradisial vocabulary applied to these three aspects of the Christian life.[13]

It is mysticism, then, that best reveals the restoration of the paradisial life. The first syndrome of this restoration is the renewed control over animals. As is well known, Adam at the beginning was told to provide names for the animals (Genesis, II, 19); for to name them is the same as to dominate them. Saint Thomas thus explained the power of Adam over creatures not endowed with reason: "The mind commands by its rule the sensitive appetites, such as the passions of anger and of desire which, in a certain way, do obey reason. *Hence* in the state of innocence, man by his command ruled over the other animals." [14] But, "both giving names and changing names played an equally important role in eschatological pronouncements. . . . The Messianic kingdom brings about a moral conversion in men and even in animals . . . conversions characteristic of the world made by the hand of God." [15] In the mystic state the animals are often subject to the saint as they were to Adam. "The history of the early Fathers of the monastic era shows—such cases are not infrequent—that they were obeyed by the wild beasts which they fed as they would domestic animals" (Dom Stolz, *op. cit.*, p. 31). Saint Francis carries on the tradition of the desert Fathers. Friendship with wild beasts and control over animals by their own consent are manifest signs of the return to a paradisial state.

In the same way we can observe the paradisial symbolism of the churches and the monastic garden. The landscape which surrounds the monk represents the earthly paradise: in a certain way it anticipates it. But it is above all the mystical experience as such which interests us. As Dom Stolz has very well shown, the typical Christian mystical experience is the ascension to Heaven of Saint Paul: "I knew a man in Christ above fourteen years ago (whether in the body, I cannot tell; or whether out of the body, I cannot tell: God knoweth;) such an one caught up to the third heaven. And I knew such a man (whether in the body or out of the body, I cannot tell: God knoweth;) How that he was caught up into paradise and heard unutterable words, which it is not lawful for a man to utter." (Second Epistle to the Corinthians, xii. 2, 3, 4.) We need not dwell here on the ascensional symbolism of Christian mysticism: in it the Ladder to Paradise plays an important role. The various degrees of contemplation are the steps in the ascent of the soul toward God. However, Saint Paul has stated precisely that this mystical ascension brings man to Paradise: the "unutterable words" which he has heard, are they not the words of God Himself? For Adam in Paradise, as Saint Gregory tells us, "delighted in frequent communion with God" (Dom Stolz, *op. cit.*, p. 111).

Accordingly, although Christianity was permeated with the yearning for Paradise, only the mystics were able to achieve its partial restoration: friendship with the animals, ascension to Heaven and meeting with God. We find the same situation in ancient religions: a certain "yearning for Paradise" appears at all levels of the religious life [16] but it shines out with greatest brilliance in the mystic experience, that is to say, in the ecstasy of the shaman. The specific characteristics of the restoration of *illud tempus* are the same: friendship with the animals, ascension to Heaven, conversation with God in Heaven. Just as does the Christian saint, the shaman in ecstasy recovers Paradise only provisionally; for neither of them can abolish death, in other terms, neither of them can re-establish the condition of primordial man.

Finally, one might remember that for Christian tradition Paradise has become all the more inaccessible because of the fire which surrounds it, or, which amounts to the same thing, because its approach is guarded by angels with flaming swords. "God," says Lactantius (*Divin. Instit.*, II, 12), "has expelled man from Paradise and surrounded it with fire so that men may no longer enter." This is what Saint Thomas means when he explains that Paradise is no longer accessible to us, principally "because of the heat which keeps it away

from our lands" (Dom Stolz, *op. cit.,* p. 24). For this reason
he who wants to enter Paradise must first cross the flames
surrounding it. "In other words, only he who has been purified by fire may thereupon enter paradise. Thus the cleansing
process precedes the mystic union, and the mystics do not hesi-
tate to put this purification of the spirit on the same level as
the purifying fire which leads to paradise. . . ." (Dom Stolz,
ibid., p. 32).

These few citations will suffice to sum up and demonstrate
the doctrine of the purifying fire which guards the entrance
to Paradise. We will not go into a discussion of the symbolism
of fire in Christian mysticism and theology. It is significant,
however, that a similar symbolism may be observed in quite
a number of shamanic techniques: witness the well-known
"mastery of fire." In fact, the shamans are always and everywhere considered "the masters of fire": during the séances
they swallow live coals, they touch the burning flame, they
tread on fire. The shamans of the earliest cultures already
bear witness to this mastery of fire; it is as much a part of
shamanism as the ecstasy, the ascent to Heaven, and the understanding of animal language. The ideology implied by
this mastery of fire is not easy to unravel: the primitive world
(indeed all popular cultures in general) makes a distinction
between the "spirits" and human beings on the ground of the
formers' "insensitivity to fire," that is to say, their ability to
resist the heat of the live coals. The shamans are said to have
got beyond the condition of man and to share in the condition of the spirits: just like spirits, they become invisible, they
fly in the air, they ascend to Heaven, they descend to Hell.
And finally they, too, enjoy "insensitivity to fire." This mastery of fire transposes their "transcendence of human conditions" into terms perceptible to the senses; here as elsewhere
the shaman proves that he has adopted a "spiritual state,"
that he has become—or may become during the séance—a
"spirit."

If one compares the purifying fire of Christian tradition
as it surrounds Paradise with the "mastery of fire" as practiced by the shamans, one notes at least one common feature:
in both cases the act of braving the fire without harm is the
sign that the human state has been overcome. But for Chris-

tianity, just as for the archaic cultures, the present state of humanity is the result of the "fall." Consequently to do away with this state, even if only provisionally, is equivalent to re-establishing the primordial condition of man, in other words, to banish time, to go backward, to recover the "paradisial" *illud tempus*. How precarious this recovery of primordial condition is, is shown, above all, by the circumstance that the shaman obtains it by imitating the state of the "spirits." We have already noted this in connection with other shamanic techniques; during the trance, it is not the shaman who flies to the Heavens but only his "spirit." A similar situation prevails in Christian mysticism: only the "soul," purified by fire, may enter Paradise.

The analogies which we have just stated seem important: it follows as a corollary that there is no break of continuity between the ideology of the "primitive" mystic experience and Judeo-Christian mysticism. Among the "primitive" peoples, just as among the saints and the Christian theologians, mystic ecstasy is a return to Paradise, expressed by the overcoming of Time and History (the "fall") and the recovery of the primordial state of Man.

Let us make it clear: in uncovering these similarities we do not pretend to make value judgments on the content of the various mystical experiences, whether "primitive" or otherwise. All we mean is that their ideologies contain as a kernel, a focal point, "the yearning for Paradise." Of course such a conclusion does not exclude the many differences between primitive and Judeo-Christian mysticism as well as those among the various schools of Christian mysticism. On the other hand, we have purposely chosen to compare Christianity and the most ancient type of mystic experience, omitting the great tradition of the East: although the "seting aside of Time" and the abolition of History are the essential elements of every mystical experience and therefore also of Eastern mysticism, it seems to us that the "paradisial" elements are better preserved in the archaic mysticisms. In certain ways, the comparisons between the forms of "primitive" mysticism and Christian mysticism have a stronger basis than those between the latter and the Indian, Chinese, and Japanese mysticisms.

Although we cannot attempt to give in these few pages a comparative study of mysticism, the chief result of our inquiry should be stressed: the complete ideological continuity between the most elementary forms of mystical experience and Christianity. At the "beginning" as well as at the "end" of the religious history of Man, we find the same "yearning for Paradise." If we take into account the fact that the "yearning for Paradise" is equally discernible in the general religious attitude of early man we have the right to assume that the mystical memory of a blessedness without history haunts man from the moment he becomes aware of his situation in the cosmos. Thus there opens a new perspective for the study of archaic anthropology. This is not the place to enter upon such a study. Suffice it to say that, in the light of all that has been noted above, certain features of "primitive" spirituality which were considered "aberrant" are not indeed to be considered as such. The imitation of animal cries by the shamans, so impressive to the observer, has at times been considered by anthropologists as manifesting a pathological "possession" whereas, on the contrary, they reveal the wish to recover friendship with animals and thus to re-establish the primordial "paradise." The ecstatic trance, no matter what its phenomenology, is "aberrant" only if its spiritual significance is disregarded. In reality, the shaman, as we have seen, is seeking to re-establish the contact between Heaven and Earth which the "fall" disrupted. The "mastery of fire" likewise is not a "savage superstition" but, on the contrary, shows how the shaman partakes of the state of the "spirits."

Viewed from its own angle, all the strange behavior of the shaman reveals the highest form of spirituality; it is actually part of a coherent ideology, possessing great nobility. The myths which make up this ideology are among the richest and most beautiful we possess, they are the myths of Paradise and the "fall," the immortality of primordial man and his communion with God; of the origin of death and of the discovery of the "spirit" (in every sense of that word). All this is not without significance for the understanding and evaluation of the "primitive" and, in general, of the nature of non-European man. Too often Western man allows himself to be moved by the *manifestation* of an ideology, while ignoring the one thing which he should know, the ideology itself, that is to say, the myths that constitute it. The *manifestations* depend on local customs and cultural styles, and the latter may or may not be directly accessible. Impression, accordingly, determines judgment: a ceremony with masks is judged "beautiful," a certain form of dance is "sinister," an initiation rite is "savage" or "aberrant." But if we take the trouble to understand the ideology which underlies all these "manifestations," if we study the myths and the symbols which condition them, we may abandon the subjectivity of "impressions" and arrive at a more objective viewpoint. At times the comprehension of the ideology is sufficient to re-establish the "normality" of a certain behavior. Recall one single example: the imitation of animal cries. For over a century, the strange cries of the shaman were felt to prove his mental aberration. But their basis was quite different: it was the yearning for Paradise, which haunted the minds of Isaiah and of Virgil, sustained the sainthood of the Fathers of the Church and came to glorious flower in the life of Saint Francis of Assisi.

NOTES

[1] Hermann Baumann, *Schoepfung und Urzeit des Menschen im Mythos Afrikanischer Voelker* (Berlin, 1936), pp. 236 *et seq.* In Africa a certain number of paradisial myths have become myths of creation; actually they explain the origin of death. Cf. Hans Abrahamson, *The Origin of Death, Studies in African Mythology,* Upsala, 1951.

[2] H. Th. Fischer, "Indonesische Paradiesmythen," *Zeitschrift fuer Ethnologie,* xiv, 1932, pp. 204-245; Franz Kiichi Numazava, *Die Weltanfaenge in der japanischen Mythologie,* Paris-Luzern, 1946.

[3] Mircea Eliade, *Le Mythe de l'Eternel Retour* (Paris, 1949), p. 21.

[4] W. Shieroszewski, "Du chamanisme d'après les croyances des Yakoutes," *Revue de l'Histoire des Religions,* xlvi, 1902.

[5] J. Castagné, "Magie et exorcisme chez les Kazak-Kirghizes et autres peuples turcs orientaux," *Revue des Etudes Islamiques,* 1930, pp. 53-151, p. 93. See also Mircea Eliade, *Le chamanisme et les techniques archaiques de l'extase* (Paris, 1951), pp. 180 *et seq.* and *passim.*

[6] T. Lehtisalo, "Beobachtungen ueber die Toder," *Journal de la Societé Finno-Ougrienne,* xlviii, 1936-1937. Eliade, "Techniques de l'extase et langages secrets," *Conferenze del Istituto italiano per il medio ed estremo Oriente,* Vol. II, 1951-1952.

[7] M. Eliade, *Le chamanisme et les techniques archaiques de l'extase,* pp. 175 *et seq.*

[8] Eliade, *ibid.*, pp. 116 *et seq.*

[9] E. Emsheimer, "Schamanentrommel und Trommelbaum," *Ethnos,* 1946, pp. 166-181; Eliade, *Le chamanisme,* pp. 159 *et seq.*

[10] Eliade, *Le chamanisme,* pp. 235 *et seq.*, 419 *et seq.;* cf. also *ibid.,* pp. 227, 295.

[11] Jean Daniélou, S. J., *Bible et Liturgie* (Paris, 1951), p. 46.

[12] *Ibid.,* p. 47.

[13] ———, *Sacramentum futuri* (Paris, 1950), p. 16.

[14] Dom Anselme Stolz, *Théologie de la mystique* (Chevetogne, 1947), p. 104.

[15] Daniélou, *op. cit.,* p. 6.

[16] Cf. Eliade, *Traité d'Histoire des religions* (Paris, 1949), pp. 321 *et seq.*

SUGGESTIONS FOR DISCUSSION

1. How well does the Paradise myth, as outlined by Eliade, answer to Murray's definitions?

2. What human needs and what characteristics of the human situation does the Paradise myth correspond to? How well suited is it to the feelings of, say, the American college student? The average factory worker?

3. How well does the analogy hold up between primitive Paradise myths and the Christian idea of Paradise?

4. What traces of the Paradise myth appear in literature of this century? Consider the novels of D. H. Lawrence, the poems of Yeats, or Faulkner's *The Bear.* What are some examples of modern literature that seem antagonistic to this myth?

5. Compare the Paradise myth with the myth of upper and lower worlds, as Frye describes it. Are the similarities or differences more striking? Can you think of a reason, from the nature of the myths themselves, why Frye's examples are mainly from sophisticated poetry and Eliade's are mainly from primitive religious tradition?

TRANSFORMATIONS OF THE HERO

JOSEPH CAMPBELL

THE PRIMORDIAL HERO AND THE HUMAN

We have come two stages: first, from the immediate emanations of the Uncreated Creating to the fluid yet timeless personages of the mythological age; second, from these Created Creating Ones to the sphere of human history. The emanations have condensed, the field of consciousness constricted. Where formerly causal bodies were visible, now only their secondary effects come to focus in the little hard-fact pupil of the human eye. The cosmogonic cycle is now to be carried forward, therefore, not by the gods, who have become invisible, but by the heroes, more or less human in character, through whom the world destiny is realized. This is the line where creation myths begin to give place to legend—as in the

---

JOSEPH CAMPBELL, born in 1904, teaches literature at Sarah Lawrence College. During his years of graduate study at Columbia and the Universities of Paris and Munich, he revived an early interest in comparative mythology, which has since remained his central concern. Among his publications are *The Hero with a Thousand Faces; A Skeleton Key to Finnegans Wake* (with H. M. Robinson); and the posthuma of Heinrich Zimmer: *Myths and Symbols in Indian Art and Civilization, The King and the Corpse, Philosophies of India,* and *The Art of Indian Asia.* He is now working on a four-volume history of mythology, entitled *The Masks of God,* of which Volume I, *Primitive Mythology,* has already appeared (The Viking Press).

Book of Genesis, following the expulsion from the garden. Metaphysics yields to prehistory, which is dim and vague at first, but becomes gradually precise in detail. The heroes become less and less fabulous, until at last, in the final stages of the various local traditions, legend opens into the common daylight of recorded time.

Mwuetsi, the Moon Man, was cut loose, like a fouled anchor; the community of the children floated free into the day-world of waking consciousness. But we are told that there existed among them direct sons of the now submarine father, who, like the children of his first begetting, had grown from infancy to manhood in a single day. These special carriers of cosmic power constituted a spiritual and social aristocracy. Filled with a double charge of the creative energy, they were themselves sources of revelation. Such figures appear on the dawn stage of every legendary past. They are the culture heroes, the city founders.

The Chinese chronicles record that when the earth had solidified and the peoples were settling in the riverlands, Fu Hsi, the "Heavenly Emperor" (2953-2838 B.C.), governed among them. He taught his tribes how to fish with nets, to hunt and to rear domestic animals, divided the people into clans, and instituted matrimony. From a supernatural tablet entrusted to him by a horse-shaped scaly monster out of the waters of the river Meng, he deduced the Eight Diagrams, which remain to this day the fundamental symbols of traditional Chinese thought. He had been born of a miraculous conception, after a gestation of twelve years; his body being that of a serpent, with human arms and the head of an ox.[1]

Shen Nung, his successor, the "Earthly Emperor" (2838-2698 B.C.), was eight feet seven inches tall, with a human body but the head of a bull. He had been miraculously conceived through the influence of a dragon. The embarrassed mother had exposed her infant on a mountainside, but the wild beasts protected and nourished it, and when she learned of this she fetched him home. Shen Nung discovered in one day seventy poisonous plants and their antidotes: through a glass covering to his stomach he could observe the digestion of each herb. Then he composed a pharmacopoeia that is still in use. He was the inventor of the plough and a system of barter; he is worshiped by the Chinese peasant as the "prince of cereals." At the age of one hundred and sixty-eight he was joined to the immortals.[2]

Such serpent kings and minotaurs tell of a past when the emperor was the carrier of a special world-creating, world-sustaining power, very much greater than that represented in the normal human physique. In those times was accomplished the heavy titan-work, the massive establishment of the foundations of our human civilization. But with the progress of the cycle, a period came when the work to be done was no longer proto- or super-human; it was the labor specifically of man—control of the passions, exploration of the arts, elaboration of the economic and cultural institutions of the state. Now is required no incarnation of the Moon Bull, no Serpent Wisdom of the Eight Diagrams of Destiny, but a perfect human spirit alert to the needs and hopes of the heart. Accordingly, the cosmogonic cycle yields an emperor in human form who shall stand for all generations to come as the model of man the king.

Huang Ti, the "Yellow Emperor" (2697-2597 B.C.), was the third of the august Three. His mother, a concubine of the prince of the province of Chao-tien, conceived him when she one night beheld a golden dazzling light around the constellation of the Great Bear. The child could talk when he was seventy days old and at the age of eleven years succeeded to the throne. His distinguishing endowment was his power to dream: in sleep he could visit the remotest regions and consort with immortals in the supernatural realm. Shortly following his elevation to the throne, Huang Ti fell into a dream that lasted three entire months, during which time he learned the lesson of the control of the heart. After a second dream of comparable length, he returned with the power to teach the people. He instructed them in the control of the forces of nature in their own hearts.

This wonderful man governed China for one hundred years, and during his reign the people enjoyed a veritable golden age. He gathered six great ministers around him, with whose help he composed a calendar, inaugurated mathematical calculations, and taught the making of utensils of wood, pottery, and metal, the building of boats and carriages, the use of money, and the construction of musical instruments of bamboo. He appointed public places for the worship of God. He instituted the bounds and laws of private property. His queen discovered the art of weaving silk. He planted one hundred varieties of grain, vegetables, and trees; favored the development of birds, quadrupeds, reptiles, and insects; taught the uses of water, fire, wood, and earth; and regulated the movements of the tides. Before his death at the age of one hundred and eleven, the phoenix and the unicorn appeared in the gardens of the Empire, in attestation to the perfection of his reign.[3]

CHILDHOOD OF THE HUMAN HERO

The earlier culture hero of the snake body and bull head carried within him from birth the spontaneous creative power of the natural world. That was the meaning of his form. The man hero, on the other hand, must "descend" to re-establish connection with the infrahuman. This is the sense, as we have seen, of the adventure of the hero.

But the makers of legend have seldom rested content to regard the world's great heroes as mere human beings who broke past the horizons that limited their fellows and returned with such boons as any man with equal faith and courage might have found. On the contrary, the tendency has always been to endow the hero with extraordinary powers from the moment of birth, or even the moment of conception. The whole hero-life is shown to have been a pageant of marvels with the great central adventure as its culmination.

This accords with the view that herohood is predestined, rather than simply achieved, and opens the problem of the relationship of biography to character. Jesus, for example, can be regarded as a man who by dint of austerities and meditation attained wisdom; or on the other hand, one may believe that a god descended and took upon himself the enactment of a human career. The first view would lead one to imitate the master literally, in order to break through, in the same way as he, to the transcendent, redemptive experience. But the second states that the hero is rather a symbol to be contemplated than an example to be literally followed. The divine being is a revelation of the omnipotent Self, which dwells within us all. The contemplation of the life thus should be undertaken as a meditation on one's own imma- nent divinity, not as a prelude to precise imitation, the lesson being, not "Do thus and be good," but "Know this and be God." [4]

In Part I, "The Adventure of the Hero," we regarded the redemptive deed from the first standpoint, which may be called the psychological. We now must describe it from the second, where it becomes a symbol of the same metaphysical mystery that it was the deed of the hero himself to rediscover and bring to view. In the present chapter, therefore, we shall consider first the miraculous childhood, by which it is shown that a special manifestation of the immanent divine principle has become incarnate in the world, and then, in succession, the various life roles through which the hero may enact his work of destiny. These vary in magnitude, according to the needs of the time.

Stated in the terms already formulated, the hero's first task is to experience consciously the antecedent stages of the cos- mogonic cycle; to break back through the epochs of emana- tion. His second, then, is to return from that abyss to the plane of contemporary life, there to serve as a human trans- former of demiurgic potentials. Huang Ti had the power to dream: this was his road of descent and return. Väinämöinen's second or water birth threw him back to an experience of the elemental. In the Tonga tale of the clam wife, the retreat began with the birth of the mother: the brother heroes sprang from an infrahuman womb.

The deeds of the hero in the second part of his personal cycle will be proportionate to the depth of his descent during the first. The sons of the clam wife came up from the animal level; their physical beauty was superlative. Väinämöinen was reborn from the elemental waters and winds; his endow- ment was to rouse or quell with bardic song the elements of nature and of the human body. Huang Ti sojourned in the kingdom of the spirit; he taught the harmony of the heart. The Buddha broke past even the zone of the creative gods and came back from the void; he announced salvation from the cosmogonic round.

If the deeds of an actual historical figure proclaim him to have been a hero, the builders of his legend will invent for him appropriate adventures in depth. These will be pictured as journeys into miraculous realms, and are to be interpreted as symbolic, on the one hand, of descents into the night-sea of the psyche, and on the other, of the realms or aspects of man's destiny that are made manifest in the respective lives.

King Sargon of Agade (c. 2550 B.C.) was born of a lowly mother. His father was unknown. Set adrift in a basket of bulrushes on the waters of the Euphrates, he was discovered by Akki the husbandman, whom he was brought up to serve as gardener. The goddess Ishtar favored the youth. Thus he became, at last, king and emperor, renowned as the living god.

Chandragupta (fourth century B.C.), the founder of the Hindu Maurya dynasty, was abandoned in an earthern jar at the threshold of a cowshed. A herdsman discovered and fostered the infant. One day when he was playing with his companions a game of High King in the Judgment Seat, little Chandragupta commanded that the worst of the offenders should have their hands and feet cut off; then, at his word, the amputated members immediately returned to place. A passing prince, beholding the miraculous game, bought the child for a thousand harshapanas and at home discovered by physical signs that he was a Maurya.

Pope Gregory the Great (A.D. 540?-604) was born of noble twins who at the instigation of the devil had committed incest. His penitent mother set him to sea in a little casket. He was found and fostered by fishermen, and at the age of six was sent to a cloister to be educated as a priest. But he desired the life of a knightly warrior. Entering a boat, he was borne miraculously to the country of his parents, where he won the hand of the queen—who presently proved to be his mother. After discovery of this second incest, Gregory remained seventeen years in penance, chained to a rock in the middle of the sea. The keys to the chains were tossed to the waters, but when at the end of the long period they were discovered in the belly of a fish, this was taken to be a providential sign: the penitent was conducted to Rome, where in due course he was elected Pope.[5]

Charlemagne (742-814) was persecuted as a child by his

elder brothers, and took flight to Saracen Spain. There, under the name of Mainet, he rendered signal services to the king. He converted the king's daughter to the Christian faith, and the two secretly arranged to marry. After further deeds, the royal youth returned to France, where he overthrew his former persecutors and triumphantly assumed the crown. Then he ruled a hundred years, surrounded by a zodiac of twelve peers. According to all reports, his beard and hair were very long and white.[6] One day, sitting under his judgment tree, he rendered justice to a snake, and in gratitude the reptile bestowed on him a charm that involved him in a love affair with a woman already dead. This amulet fell into a well at Aix: that is why Aix became the emperor's favorite residence. After his long wars against the Saracens, Saxons, Slavs, and Northmen, the ageless emperor died; but he sleeps only, to awake in the hour of his country's need. During the later Middle Ages, he once arose from the dead to participate in a crusade.[7]

Each of these biographies exhibits the variously rationalized theme of the infant exile and return. This is a prominent feature in all legend, folk tale, and myth. Usually an effort is made to give it some semblance of physical plausibility. However, when the hero in question is a great patriarch, wizard, prophet, or incarnation, the wonders are permitted to develop beyond all bounds.

The popular Hebrew legend of the birth of father Abraham supplies an example of the frankly supernatural infant exile. The event of the birth had been read by Nimrod in the stars, "for this impious king was a cunning astrologer, and it was manifest to him that a man would be born in his day who would rise up against him and triumphantly give the lie to his religion. In his terror at the fate foretold in the stars, he sent for his princes and governors, and asked them to advise him in the matter. They answered, and said: 'Our unanimous advice is that thou shouldst build a great house, station a guard at the entrance thereof, and make known in the whole of thy realm that all pregnant women shall repair thither together with their midwives, who are to remain with them when they are delivered. When the days of a woman to be delivered are fulfilled, and the child is born, it shall be the duty of the midwife to kill it, if it be a boy. But if the child be a girl, it shall be kept alive, and the mother shall receive gifts and costly garments, and a herald shall proclaim, "Thus is done unto the woman who bears a daughter!" '

"The king was pleased with this counsel, and he had a proclamation published throughout his whole kingdom, summoning all the architects to build a great house for him, sixty ells high and eighty wide. After it was completed, he issued a second proclamation, summoning all pregnant women thither, and there they were to remain until their confinement. Officers were appointed to take the women to the house, and guards were stationed in it and about it, to prevent the women from escaping thence. He furthermore sent midwives to the house, and commanded them to slay the men children at their mothers' breasts. But if a woman bore a girl, she was to be arrayed in byssus, silk, and embroidered garments, and led forth from the house of detention amid great honors. No less than seventy thousand children were slaughtered thus. Then the angels appeared before God, and spoke, 'Seest Thou not what he doth, yon sinner and blasphemer, Nimrod son of Canaan, who slays so many innocent babes that have done no harm?' God answered, and said: 'Ye holy angels, I know it and I see it, for I neither slumber nor sleep. I behold and I know the secret things and the things that are revealed, and ye shall witness what I will do unto this sinner and blasphemer, for I will turn My hand against him to chastise him.'

"It was about this time that Terah espoused the mother of Abraham and she was with child. . . . When her time approached, she left the city in great terror and wandered toward the desert, walking along the edge of a valley, until she happened across a cave. She entered this refuge, and on the next day she was seized with the throes, and she gave birth to a son. The whole cave was filled with the light of the child's countenance as with the splendor of the sun, and the mother rejoiced exceedingly. The babe she bore was our father Abraham.

"His mother lamented, and said to her son: 'Alas that I bore thee at a time when Nimrod is king. For thy sake seventy thousand men-children were slaughtered, and I am seized with terror on account of thee, that he hear of thy existence, and slay thee. Better thou shouldst perish here in this cave than my eye should behold thee dead at my breast.' She took the garment in which she was clothed, and wrapped it about the boy. Then she abandoned him in the cave, saying, 'May the Lord be with thee, may He not fail thee nor forsake thee.'

"Thus Abraham was deserted in the cave, without a nurse, and he began to wail. God sent Gabriel down to give him milk to drink, and the angel made it to flow from the little finger of the baby's right hand, and he sucked it until he was ten days old. Then he arose and walked about, and he left the cave and went along the edge of the valley. When the sun sank, and the stars came forth, he said, 'These are the gods!' But the dawn came, and the stars could be seen no longer, and then he said, 'I will not pay worship to these, for they are no gods.' Thereupon the sun came forth, and he spoke, 'This is my god, him will I extol.' But again the sun set and he said, 'He is no god,' and beholding the moon, he called him his god to whom he would pay divine homage. Then the moon was obscured, and he cried out: This, too, is no god! There is One who sets them all in motion.' " [8]

The Blackfeet of Montana tell of a young monster-slayer, Kut-o-yis, who was discovered by his foster parents when the old man and woman put a clot of buffalo blood to boil in a pot. "Immediately there came from the pot a noise as of a child crying, as if it were being hurt, burnt, or scalded. They looked in the kettle, and saw there a little boy, and they quickly took it out of the water. They were very much surprised. . . . Now on the fourth day the child spoke, and said, 'Lash me in turn to each of these lodge poles, and when I get to the last one, I shall fall out of my lashing and be grown up.' The old woman did so, and as she lashed him to each lodge pole he could be seen to grow, and finally when they lashed him to the last pole, he was a man." [9]

The folk tales commonly support or supplant this theme of the exile with that of the despised one, or the handicapped: the abused youngest son or daughter, the orphan, stepchild, ugly duckling, or the squire of low degree.

A young Pueblo woman, who was helping her mother mix

clay for pottery with her foot, felt a splash of mud on her leg
but thought no more of it. "After some days the girl felt
something was moving in her belly, but she did not think
anything about going to have a baby. She did not tell her
mother. But it was growing and growing. One day in the
morning she was very sick. In the afternoon she got the baby.
Then her mother knew (for the first time) that her daughter
was going to have a baby. The mother was very angry about
it; but after she looked at the baby, she saw it was not like a
baby, she saw it was a round thing with two things sticking
out, it was a little jar. "Where did you get this?' said her
mother. The girl was just crying. About that time the father
came in. 'Never mind, I am very glad she had a baby,' he said.
'But it is not a baby,' said her mother. Then the father went
to look at it and saw it was a little water jar. After that he
was very fond of that little jar. 'It is moving,' he said. Pretty
soon that little water jar was growing. In twenty days it was
big. It was able to go around with the children, and it could
talk. 'Grandfather, take me outdoors, so I can look around,'
he said. So every morning the grandfather would take him
out and he would look at the children, and they were very
fond of him and they found out he was a boy, Water Jar boy.
They found out from his talking." [10]

In sum: the child of destiny has to face a long period of
obscurity. This is a time of extreme danger, impediment, or
disgrace. He is thrown inward to his own depths or outward
to the unknown; either way, what he touches is a darkness
unexplored. And this is a zone of unsuspected presences, be-
nign as well as malignant: an angel appears, a helpful animal,
a fisherman, a hunter, crone, or peasant. Fostered in the animal school, or, like Siegfried, below ground among the
gnomes that nourish the roots of the tree of life, or again,
alone in some little room (the story has been told a thousand
ways), the young world-apprentice learns the lesson of the
seed powers, which reside just beyond the sphere of the meas-
ured and the named.

The myths agree that an extraordinary capacity is required
to face and survive such experience. The infancies abound in
anecdotes of precocious strength, cleverness, and wisdom.
Herakles strangled a serpent sent against his cradle by the

goddess Hera. Maui of Polynesia snared and slowed the sun—to give his mother time to cook her meals. Abraham, as we have seen, arrived at the knowledge of the One God. Jesus confounded the wise men. The baby Buddha had been left one day beneath the shade of a tree; his nurses suddenly noted that the shadow had not moved all afternoon and that the child was sitting fixed in a yogic trance.

The feats of the beloved Hindu savior, Krishna, during his infant exile among the cowherds of Gokula and Brindaban, constitute a lively cycle. A certain goblin named Putana came in the shape of a beautiful woman, but with poison in her breasts. She entered the house of Yasoda, the foster mother of the child, and made herself very friendly, presently taking the baby in her lap to give it suck. But Krishna drew so hard that he sucked away her life, and she fell dead, reassuming her huge and hideous form. When the foul corpse was cremated, however, it emitted a sweet fragrance; for the divine infant had given the demoness salvation when he had drunk her milk.

Krishna was a mischievous little boy. He liked to spirit away the pots of curds when the milkmaids were asleep. He was forever climbing to eat and spill things placed out of his reach on the high shelves. The girls would call him Butter-thief and complain to Yasoda; but he could always invent a story. One afternoon when he was playing in the yard, his foster parent was warned that he was eating clay. She arrived with a switch, but he had wiped his lips, and denied all knowledge of the matter. She opened the dirty mouth to see, but when she peered inside beheld the whole universe, the "Three Worlds." She thought: "How silly I am to imagine that my son could be the Lord of the Three Worlds." Then all was veiled from her again, and the moment passed immediately from her mind. She fondled the little boy and took him home.

The herding folk were accustomed to pay worship to the god Indra, the Hindu counterpart of Zeus, king of heaven and lord of rain. One day when they had made their offering, the lad Krishna said to them: "Indra is no supreme deity, though he be king in heaven; he is afraid of the titans. Furthermore, the rain and prosperity for which you are praying

depend on the sun, which draws up the waters and makes
them fall again. What can Indra do? Whatever comes to pass
is determined by the laws of nature and the spirit." Then he
turned their attention to the nearby woods, streams, and hills,
and especially to Mount Govardhan, as more worthy of their
honor than the remote master of the air. And so they offered
flowers and fruits and sweetmeats to the mountain.

Krishna himself assumed a second form: he took the form
of a mountain god and received the offerings of the people,
meanwhile remaining in his earlier shape among them, pay-
ing worship to the mountain king. The god received the
offerings and ate them up.[11]

Indra was enraged, and sent for the king of the clouds,
whom he commanded to pour rain over the people until all
should be swept away. A flight of storm clouds drew over the
district and began to discharge a deluge; it seemed the end of
the world was at hand. But the lad Krishna filled Mount Govardhan with the heat of his inexhaustible energy, lifted it
with his little finger, and bid the people take shelter beneath.
The rain struck the mountain, hissed, and evaporated. The
torrent fell seven days, but not a drop touched the community
of herdsmen.

Then the god realized that the opponent must be an incarnation of the Primal Being. When Krishna went out next
day to graze the cows, playing music on his flute, the King of
Heaven came down on his great white elephant, Airavata, fell
on his face at the feet of the smiling lad, and made submission.[12]

The conclusion of the childhood cycle is the return or recognition of the hero, when, after the long period of obscurity,
his true character is revealed. This event may precipitate a
considerable crisis; for it amounts to an emergence of powers
hitherto excluded from human life. Earlier patterns break to
fragments or dissolve; disaster greets the eye. Yet after a moment of apparent havoc, the creative value of the new factor
comes to view, and the world takes shape again in unsuspected glory. This theme of crucifixion-resurrection can be
illustrated either on the body of the hero himself, or in his
effects upon his world. The first alternative we find in the
Pueblo story of the water jar.

"The men were going out to hunt rabbits, and Water Jar boy wanted to go. 'Grandfather, could you take me down to the foot of the mesa, I want to hunt rabbits.' 'Poor grandson, you can't hunt rabbits, you have no legs or arms,' said the grandfather. But Water Jar boy was very anxious to go. 'Take me anyway. You are too old and you can't do anything.' His mother was crying because her boy had no legs or arms or eyes. But they used to feed him, in his mouth, in the mouth of the jar. So next morning his grandfather took him down to the south on the flat. Then he rolled along, and pretty soon he saw a rabbit track and he followed the track. Pretty soon the rabbit ran out, and he began to chase it. Just before he got to the marsh there was a rock, and he hit himself against it and broke, and a boy jumped up. He was very glad his skin had been broken and that he was a boy, a big boy. He was wearing lots of beads around his neck and turquoise earrings, and a dance kilt and moccasins, and a buckskin shirt." Catching a number of rabbits, he returned and presented them to his grandfather, who brought him triumphantly home.[13]

The cosmic energies burning within the vivid Irish warrior Cuchulainn—chief hero of the medieval Ulster Cycle, the so-called "Cycle of the Knights of the Red Branch" [14]—would suddenly burst like an eruption, both overwhelming himself and smashing everything around. When he was four years old —so the story goes—he set out to test the "boy corps" of his uncle, King Conchobar, at their own sports. Carrying his hurly of brass, ball of silver, throwing javelin, and toy spear, he proceeded to the court city of Emania, where, without so much as a word of permission, he dived right in among the boys—"thrice fifty in number, who were hurling on the green and practicing martial exercises with Conchobar's son, Follamain, at their head." The whole field let fly at him. With his fists, forearms, palms, and little shield, he parried the hurlies, balls, and spears that came simultaneously from all directions. Then for the first time in his life he was seized with his battle-frenzy (a bizarre, characteristic transformation later to be known as his "paroxysm" or "distortion") and before anyone could grasp what was coming to pass, he had laid low fifty of the best. Five more of the boy corps went scuttling

past the king, where he sat playing chess with Fergus the Eloquent. Conchobar arose and took a hand in the confusion.
But Cuchulainn would not lighten his hand until all the
youngsters had been placed under his protection and guar-
antee.[15]

Cuchulainn's first day under arms was the occasion of his
full self-manifestation. There was nothing serenely controlled
about this performance, nothing of the playful irony that we
feel in the deeds of the Hindu Krishna. Rather, the abundance of Cuchulainn's power was becoming known for the
first time to himself, as well as to everybody else. It broke out
of the depths of his being, and then had to be dealt with, im-
promptu and fast.

The happening was again at the court of King Conchobar,
the day Cathbad the Druid declared in prophecy of any strip-
ling who that day should assume arms and armature that
"the name of such an one would transcend those of all Ireland's youths besides: his life however would be fleeting
short." Cuchulainn forthwith demanded fighting equipment.
Seventeen sets of weapons given him he shattered with his
strength, until Conchobar invested him with his own outfit.
Then he reduced the chariots to fragments. Only that of the
king was strong enough to support his trial.

Cuchulainn commanded Conchobar's charioteer to drive
him past the distant "Look-out Ford," and they came presently to a remote fortress, the Dun of the Sons of Nechtan,
where he cut off the heads of the defenders. He fastened the
heads to the sides of the car. On the road back he jumped to
the ground and "by sheer running and mere speed" captured
two stags of the grandest bulk. With two stones he knocked
out of the air two dozen flying swans. And with thongs and
other gear he tethered all, both the beasts and the birds, to
the chariot.

Levarchan the Prophetess beheld the pageant with alarm
as it approached the city and castle of Emania. "The chariot
is graced with bleeding heads of his enemies," she declared,
"beautiful white birds he has which in the chariot bear him
company, and wild unbroken stags bound and tethered to the
same." "I know that chariot-fighter," the king said: "even
the little boy, my sister's son, who this very day went to the

marches. Surely he will have reddened his hand; and should his fury not be timely met, all Emania's young men will perish by him." Very quickly, a method had to be contrived to abate his heat; and one was found. One hundred and fifty women of the castle, and Scandlach their leader at the head of them, "reduced themselves critically to nature's garb, and without subterfuge of any kind trooped out to meet him." The little warrior, embarrassed or perhaps overwhelmed by such a display of womanhood, averted his eyes, at which moment he was seized by the men and soused into a vat of cold water. The staves and hoops of the vessel flew asunder. A second vat boiled. The third became only very hot. Thus Cuchulainn was subdued, and the city saved.[16]

"A beautiful boy indeed was that: seven toes to each foot Cuchulainn had, and to either hand as many fingers; his eyes were bright with seven pupils apiece, each one of which glittered with seven gemlike sparkles. On either cheek he had four moles: a blue, a crimson, a green, and a yellow. Between one ear and the other he had fifty clear-yellow long tresses that were as the yellow wax of bees, or like unto a brooch of the white gold as it glints to the sun unobscured. He wore a green mantle silver-clasped upon his breast and a gold-thread shirt." [17] But when he was taken by his paroxysm or distortion "he became a fearsome and multiform and wondrous and hitherto unknown being." All over him, from his crown to the ground, his flesh and every limb and joint and point and articulation of him quivered. His feet, shins, and knees shifted themselves and were behind him. The frontal sinews of his head were dragged to the back of his neck, where they showed in lumps bigger than the head of a man-child aged one month. "One eye became engulfed in his head so far that 'tis a question whether a wild heron could have got at it where it lay against his occiput, to drag it out upon the surface of his cheek; the other eye on the contrary protruded suddenly, and of itself so rested upon the cheek. His mouth was twisted awry till it met his ears . . . flakes of fire streamed from it. The sounding blows of the heart that pounded within him were as the howl of a ban-dog doing his office, or of a lion in the act of charging bears. Among the aërial clouds over his head were visible the virulent pouring showers and sparks of

ruddy fire which the seething of his savage wrath caused to
mount up above him. His hair became tangled about his
head . . . over the which though a prime apple-tree had been
shaken, yet may we surmise that never an apple of them
would have reached the ground, but rather that all would
have been held impaled each on an individual hair as it
bristled on him for fury. His 'hero's paroxysm' projected itself out of his forehead, and showed longer as well as thicker
than the whetstone of a first-rate man-at-arms. [And finally:]
taller, thicker, more rigid, longer than the mast of a great
ship was the perpendicular jet of dusky blood which out of
his scalp's very central point shot upwards and then was scattered to the four cardinal points; whereby was formed a
magic mist of gloom resembling the smoky pall that drapes
a regal dwelling, what time a king at night fall of a winter's
day draws near to it." [18]

THE HERO AS WARRIOR

The place of the hero's birth, or the remote land of exile from
which he returns to perform his adult deeds among men, is
the mid-point or navel of the world. Just as ripples go out
from an underwater spring, so the forms of the universe ex-
pand in circles from this source.

"Above the broad, unmoving depths, beneath the nine
spheres and the seven floors of heaven, at the central point,
the World Navel, the quietest place on the earth, where the
moon does not wane, nor the sun go down, where eternal
summer rules and the cuckoo everlastingly calls, there the
White Youth came to consciousness." So begins a hero myth
of the Yakuts of Siberia. The White Youth went forth to
learn where he was and what his dwelling place was like.
Eastward of him lay stretching a broad, fallow field, in the
middle of which arose a mighty hill, and on the summit of
the hill a gigantic tree. The resin of that tree was transparent
and sweet scented, the bark never dried or cracked, the sap
shone silver, the luxuriant leaves never wilted, and the cat-
kins resembled a cluster of reversed cups. The summit of the
tree rose over the seven heaven-floors and served as a tether-
ing post for the High God, Yryn-ai-tojon; while the roots

penetrated into subterranean abysses, where they formed the pillars of the dwellings of the mythical creatures proper to that zone. The tree held conversation, through its foliage, with the beings of the sky.

When the White Youth turned to face south, he perceived in the midst of a green grassy plain the quiet Lake of Milk that no breath of wind ever stirs; and around the shores of the lake were swamps of curdle. To the north of him a somber forest stood with trees that rustled day and night; and therein was moving every kind of beast. Tall mountains were lifting beyond it, and appeared to be wearing caps of white rabbit fur; they leaned against the sky and protected this middle place from the northern wind. A thicket of scrub stretched out to the west, and beyond it stood a forest of tall firs; behind the forest gleamed a number of blunt-headed solitary peaks.

This was the manner, then, of the world in which the White Youth beheld the light of day. Presently tired, however, of being alone, he went over to the gigantic tree of life. "Honored High Mistress, Mother of my Tree and my Dwelling Place," he prayed; "everything that lives exists in pairs and propagates descendants, but I am alone. I want now to travel and to seek a wife of my own kind; I wish to measure my strength against my kind; I want to become acquainted with men—to live according to the manner of men. Do not deny me thy blessing; I do humbly pray. I bow my head and bend my knee."

Then the leaves of the tree began murmuring, and a fine, milk-white rain descended from them upon the White Youth. A warm breath of wind could be felt. The tree began to groan, and out of its roots a female figure emerged to the waist: a woman of middle age, with earnest regard, hair flowing free, and bosom bare. The goddess offered her milk to the youth from a sumptuous breast, and after partaking of it he felt his strength increase a hundred-fold. At the same time the goddess promised the youth every happiness and blessed him in such a way that neither water, nor fire, iron, nor anything else should ever do him harm.[19]

From the umbilical spot the hero departs to realize his destiny. His adult deeds pour creative power into the world.

Sang the aged Väinämöinen;
Lakes swelled up, and earth was shaken,
And the coppery mountains trembled,
And the mighty rocks resounded.
And the mountains clove asunder;
On the shore the stones were shattered.[20]

The stanza of the hero-bard resounds with the magic of the word of power; similarly, the sword edge of the hero-warrior flashes with the energy of the creative Source: before it fall the shells of the Outworn.

For the mythological hero is the champion not of things become but of things becoming; the dragon to be slain by him is precisely the monster of the status quo: Holdfast, the keeper of the past. From obscurity the hero emerges, but the enemy is great and conspicuous in the seat of power; he is enemy, dragon, tyrant, because he turns to his own advantage the authority of his position. He is Holdfast not because he keeps the *past* but because he *keeps.*

The tyrant is proud, and therin resides his doom. He is proud because he thinks of his strength as his own; thus he is in the clown role, as a mistaker of shadow for substance; it is his destiny to be tricked. The mythological hero, reappearing from the darkness that is the source of the shapes of the day, brings a knowledge of the secret of the tyrant's doom. With a gesture as simple as the pressing of a button, he annihilates the impressive configuration. The hero-deed is a continuous shattering of the crystallizations of the moment. The cycle rolls: mythology focuses on the growing-point. Transformation, fluidity, not stubborn ponderosity, is the characteristic of the living God. The great figure of the moment exists only to be broken, cut into chunks, and scattered abroad. Briefly: the ogre-tyrant is the champion of the prodigious fact, the hero the champion of creative life.

The world period of the hero in *human* form begins only when villages and cities have expanded over the land. Many monsters remaining from primeval times still lurk in the outlying regions, and through malice or desperation these set themselves against the human community. They have to be cleared away. Furthermore, tyrants of human breed, usurping to themselves the goods of their neighbors, arise, and are the cause of widespread misery. These have to be suppressed. The elementary deeds of the hero are those of the clearing of the field.[21]

Kut-o-yis, or "Blood Clot Boy," when he had been taken from the pot and had grown to manhood in a day, slew the murderous son-in-law of his foster parents, then proceeded against the ogres of the countryside. He exterminated a tribe of cruel bears, with the exception of one female who was about to become a mother. "She pleaded so pitifully for her life, that he spared her. If he had not done this, there would have been no bears in the world." Then he slaughtered a tribe of snakes, but again with the exception of one "who was about to become a mother." Next he deliberately walked along a road which he had been told was dangerous. "As he was going along, a great windstorm struck him and at last carried him into the mouth of a great fish. This was a sucker-fish and the wind was its sucking. When he got into the stomach of the fish, he saw a great many people. Many of them were dead, but some were still alive. He said to the people, 'Ah, there must be a heart somewhere here. We will have a dance.' So he painted his face white, his eyes and mouth with black circles, and tied a white rock knife on his head, so that the point stuck up. Some rattles made of hoofs were also brought. Then the people started in to dance. For a while Blood Clot sat making wing-motions with his hands, and singing songs. Then he stood up and danced, jumping up and down until the knife on his head struck the heart. Then he cut the heart down. Next he cut through between the ribs of the fish, and let all the people out.

"Again Blood Clot said he must go on his travels. Before starting, the people warned him, saying that after a while he would see a woman who was always challenging people to wrestle with her, but that he must not speak to her. He gave no heed to what they said, and, after he had gone a little way, he saw a woman who called him to come over. 'No,' said Blood Clot. 'I am in a hurry.' However, at the fourth time the woman asked him to come over, he said, 'Yes, but you must wait a little while, for I am tired. I wish to rest. When I have rested, I will come over and wrestle with you.' Now, while he was resting, he saw many large knives sticking up from the ground almost hidden by straw. Then he knew that the woman killed the people she wrestled with by throwing them down on the knives. When he was rested, he went on. The woman asked him to stand up in the place where he had seen the knives; but he said, 'No, I am not quite ready. Let us play a little, before we begin.' So he began to play with the woman, but quickly caught hold of her, threw her upon the knives, and cut her in two.

"Blood Clot took up his travels again, and after a while came to a camp where there were some old women. The old women told him that a little farther on he would come to a woman with a swing, but on no account must he ride with her. After a time he came to a place where he saw a swing on the bank of a swift stream. There was a woman swinging on it. He watched her a while, and saw that she killed people by swinging them out and dropping them into the water. When he found this out, he came up to the woman. 'You have a swing here; let me see you swing,' he said. 'No,' said the woman, 'I want to see you swing.' 'Well,' said Blood Clot, 'but you must swing first.' 'Well,' said the woman, 'now I shall swing. Watch me. Then I shall see you do it.' So the woman swung out over the stream. As she did this, he saw how it worked. Then he said to the woman, 'You swing again while I am getting ready'; but as the woman swung out this time, he cut the vine and let her drop into the water. This happened on Cut Bank Creek." [22]

We are familiar with such deeds from our Jack-the-Giant-Killer nursery tales and the classical accounts of the labors of such heroes as Herakles and Theseus. They abound also in the legends of the Christian saints, as in the following charming French tale of Saint Martha.

"There was at that time on the banks of the Rhône, in a forest situated between Avignon and Arles, a dragon, half animal, half fish, larger than an ox, longer than a horse, with teeth as sharp as horns, and great wings at either side of its body; and this monster slew all the travelers and sank all the boats. It had arrived by sea from Galatia. Its parents were the Leviathan—a monster in the form of a serpent that dwelt in the sea—and the Onager—a terrible beast bred in Galatia, which burns with fire everything it touches.

"Now Saint Martha, at the earnest request of the people, went against the dragon. Having found it in the forest, in the act of devouring a man, she sprinkled holy water on it and exhibited a crucifix. Immediately, the monster, vanquished, came like a lamb to the side of the saint, who passed her belt around its neck and conducted it to the neighboring village. There the populace slew it with stones and staffs.

"And since the dragon had been known to the people under the name of Tarasque, the town took the name of Tarascon, in remembrance. Up to then it had been called Nerluc, which is to say, Black Lake, on acount of the somber forests which there bordered the stream." [23]

The warrior-kings of antiquity regarded their work in the spirit of the monster-slayer. This formula, indeed, of the shining hero going against the dragon has been the great device of self-justification for all crusades. Numberless memorial tablets have been composed with the grandiose complacency of the following cuneiform of Sargon of Agade, destroyer of the ancient cities of the Sumerians, from whom his own people had derived their civilization.

"Sargon, king of Agade, viceregent of the goddess Ishtar, king of Kish, *pashishu* [24] of the god Anu, King of the Land, great *ishakku* [25] of the god Enlil: the city of Uruk he smote and its wall he destroyed. With the people of Uruk, he battled and he captured him and in fetters led him through the gate of Enlil. Sargon, king of Agade, battled with the man of Ur and vanquished him; his city he smote and its wall he destroyed. E-Ninmar he smote and its wall he destroyed, and its entire territory, from Lagash to the sea, he smote. His weapons he washed in the sea. . . ."

THE HERO AS WORLD REDEEMER

Two degrees of initiation are to be distinguished in the mansion of the father. From the first the son returns as emissary, but from the second, with the knowledge that "I and the father are one." Heroes of this second, highest illumination are the world redeemers, the so-called incarnations, in the highest sense. Their myths open out to cosmic proportions.

Their words carry an authority beyond anything pronounced by the heroes of the scepter and the book.

"All of you watch me. Don't look around," said the hero of the Jicarilla Apache, Killer-of-Enemies; "Listen to what I say. The world is just as big as my body. The world is as large as my word. And the world is as large as my prayers. The sky is only as large as my words and prayers. The seasons are only as great as my body, my words, and my prayer. It is the same with the waters; my body, my words, my prayer are greater than the waters.

"Whoever believes me, whoever listens to what I say, will have long life. One who doesn't listen, who thinks in some evil way, will have a short life.

"Don't think I am in the east, south, west, or north. The earth is my body. I am there. I am all over. Don't think I stay only under the earth or up in the sky, or only in the seasons, or on the other side of the waters. These are all my body. It is the truth that the underworld, the sky, the seasons, the waters, are all my body. I am all over.

"I have already given you that with which you have to make an offering to me. You have two kinds of pipe and you have the mountain tobacco." [26]

The work of the incarnation is to refute by his presence the pretensions of the tyrant ogre. The latter has occluded the source of grace with the shadow of his limited personality; the incarnation, utterly free of such ego-consciousness, is a direct manifestation of the law. On a grandiose scale he enacts the hero-life—performs the hero-deeds, slays the monster—but it is all with the freedom of a work done only to make evident to the eye what might have been accomplished equally well with a mere thought.

Kans, the cruel uncle of Krishna, usurper of his own father's throne in the city of Mathura, heard a voice one day that said to him: "Thy enemy is born, thy death is certain." Krishna and his elder brother Balarama had been spirited to the cowherds from their mother's womb to protect them from this Indian counterpart of Nimrod. And he had sent demons after them—Putana of the poison milk was the first—but all had been undone. Now when his devices had failed, Kans determined to lure the youths to his city. A messenger was

sent to invite the cowherds to a sacrifice and great tournament. The invitation was accepted. With the brothers among
them, the cowherds came and camped outside the city wall.

Krishna and Balarama, his brother, went in to see the wonders of the town. There were great gardens, palaces, and
groves. They encountered a washerman and asked him for
some fine clothes; when he laughed and refused, they took
the clothes by force and made themselves very gay. Then a
hump-backed woman prayed Krishna to let her rub sandal-
paste on his body. He went up to her, placing his feet on
hers, and with two fingers beneath her chin, lifted her up
and made her straight and fair. And he said: "When I have
slain Kans I shall come back and be with you."

The brothers came to the empty stadium. There the bow
of the god Shiva was set up, huge as three palm trees, great
and heavy. Krishna advanced to the bow, pulled it, and it
broke with a mighty noise. Kans in his palace heard the
sound and was appalled.

The tyrant sent his troops to kill the brothers in the city.
But the lads slew the soldiers and returned to their camp.
They told the cowherds they had had an interesting tour,
then ate their suppers, and went to bed.

Kans that night had ominous dreams. When he woke, he
ordered the stadium prepared for the tournament and the
trumpets blown for assembly. Krishna and Balarama arrived
as jugglers, followed by the cowherds, their friends. When
they entered the gate, there was a furious elephant ready to
crush them, mighty as ten thousand common elephants. The
driver rode it directly at Krishna. Balarama gave it such a
blow with his fist that it halted, started back. The driver rode
it again, but the two brothers struck it to the ground, and
it was dead.

The youths walked onto the field. Everybody saw what his
own nature revealed to him: the wrestlers thought Krishna
a wrestler, the women thought him the treasure of beauty,
the gods knew him as their lord, and Kans thought he was
Mara, Death himself. When he had undone every one of the
wrestlers sent against him, slaying finally the strongest, he
leapt to the royal dais, dragged the tyrant by the hair, and
killed him. Men, gods, and saints were delighted, but the

king's wives came forth to mourn. Krishna, seeing their grief, comforted them with his primal wisdom: "Mother," he said, "do not grieve. No one can live and not die. To imagine oneself as possessing anything is to be mistaken; nobody is father, mother, or son. There is only the continuous round of birth and death." [27]

The legends of the redeemer describe the period of desolation as caused by a moral fault on the part of man (Adam in the garden, Jemshid on the throne). Yet from the standpoint of the cosmogonic cycle, a regular alternation of fair and foul is characteristic of the spectacle of time. Just as in the history of the universe, so also in that of nations: emanation leads to dissolution, youth to age, birth to death, form-creative vitality to the dead weight of inertia. Life surges, precipitating forms, and then ebbs, leaving jetsam behind. The golden age, the reign of the world emperor, alternates, in the pulse of every moment of life, with the waste land, the reign of the tyrant. The god who is the creator becomes the destroyer in the end.

From this point of view the tyrant ogre is no less representative of the father than the earlier world emperor whose position he usurped, or than the brilliant hero (the son) who is to supplant him. He is the representative of the set-fast, as the hero is the carrier of the changing. And since every moment of time bursts free from the fetters of the moment before, so this dragon, Holdfast, is pictured as of the generation immediately preceding that of the savior of the world.

Stated in direct terms: the work of the hero is to slay the tenacious aspect of the father (dragon, tester, ogre king) and release from its ban the vital energies that will feed the universe. "This can be done either in accordance with the Father's will or against his will; he [the Father] may 'choose death for his children's sake,' or it may be that the Gods impose the passion upon him, making him their sacrificial victim. These are not contradictory doctrines, but different ways of telling one and the same story; in reality, Slayer and Dragon, sacrificer and victim, are of one mind behind the scenes, where there is no polarity of contraries, but mortal enemies on the stage, where the everlasting war of the Gods and the Titans is displayed. In any case, the Dragon-Father remains a Pleroma, no more diminished by what he exhales than he is increased by what he repossesses. He is the Death, on whom our life depends; and to the question 'Is Death one, or many?' the answer is made that 'He is one as he is there, but many as he is in his children here.' " [28]

The hero of yesterday becomes the tyrant of tomorrow, unless he crucifies *himself* today.

From the point of view of the present there is such a recklessness in this deliverance of the future that it appears to be nihilistic. The words of Krishna, the world savior, to the wives of the dead Kans carry a frightening overtone; so do the words of Jesus: "I came not to send peace, but a sword. For I am come to set a man at variance against his father, and the daughter against her mother, and the daughter-in-law against her mother-in-law. And a man's foes shall be they of his own household. He that loveth father or mother more than me is not worthy of me: and he that loveth son or daughter more than me is not worthy of me." [29] To protect the unprepared, mythology veils such ultimate revelations under half-obscuring guises, while yet insisting on the gradually instructive form. The savior figure who eliminates the tyrant father and then himself assumes the crown is (like Oedipus) stepping into his sire's stead. To soften the harsh patricide, the legend represents the father as some cruel uncle or usurping Nimrod. Nevertheless, the half-hidden fact remains. Once it is glimpsed, the entire spectacle buckles: the son slays the father, but the son and the father are one. The enigmatical figures dissolve back into the primal chaos. This is the wisdom of the end (and rebeginning) of the world.

DEPARTURE OF THE HERO

The last act in the biography of the hero is that of the death or departure. Here the whole sense of the life is epitomized. Needless to say, the hero would be no hero if death held for him any terror; the first condition is reconciliation with the grave.

"While sitting under the oak of Mamre, Abraham perceived a flashing of light and a smell of sweet odor, and turning around he saw Death coming toward him in great glory and beauty. And Death said unto Abraham: 'Think not, Abraham, that this beauty is mine, or that I come thus to every man. Nay, but if any one is righteous like thee, I thus take a crown and come to him, but if he is a sinner, I come in great corruption, and out of their sins I make a crown for my head, and I shake them with great fear, so that they are dismayed.' Abraham said to him, 'And art thou, indeed, he that is called Death?' He answered, and said, 'I am the bitter name,' but Abraham answered, 'I will not go with thee.' And Abraham said to Death, 'Show us thy corruption.' And Death revealed his corruption, showing two heads, the one had the face of a serpent, the other head was like a sword. All the servants of Abraham, looking at the fierce mien of Death, died, but Abraham prayed to the Lord, and he raised them up. As the looks of Death were not able to cause Abraham's soul to depart from him, God removed the soul of Abraham as in a dream, and the archangel Michael took it up into heaven. After great praise and glory had been given to the Lord by the angels who brought Abraham's soul, and after Abraham bowed down to worship, then came the voice of God, saying thus: 'Take My friend Abraham into Paradise, where are the tabernacles of My righteous ones and the abodes of My saints Isaac and Jacob in his bosom, where there is no trouble, nor grief, nor sighing, but peace and rejoicing and life unending.' " [30]

Compare the following dream. "I was on a bridge where I met a blind fiddler. Everyone was tossing coins into his hat. I came closer and perceived that the musician was not blind. He had a squint, and was looking at me with a crooked glance from the side. Suddenly, there was a little old woman sitting at the side of a road. It was dark and I was afraid. 'Where does this road lead?' I thought. A young peasant came along the road and took me by the hand. 'Do you want to come home,' he said, 'and drink coffee?' 'Let me go! You are holding too tight!' I cried, and awoke." [31]

The hero, who in his life represented the dual perspective, after his death is still a synthesizing image: like Charlemagne, he sleeps only and will arise in the hour of destiny, or he is among us under another form.

The Aztecs tell of the feathered serpent, Quetzalcoatl, monarch of the ancient city of Tollan in the golden age of its prosperity. He was the teacher of the arts, originator of the calendar, and the giver of maize. He and his people were overcome, at the close of their time, by the stronger magic of an invading race, the Aztecs. Tezcatlipoca, the warrior-hero of the younger people and their era, broke the city of Tollan; and the feathered serpent, king of the golden age, burned his dwellings behind him, buried his treasures in the mountains, transformed his chocolate trees into mesquite, commanded the multi-colored birds, his servants, to fly before him, and departed in great sorrow. And he came to a city called Qua-uhtitlan, where there was a tree, very tall and large; and he went over to the tree, sat down beneath it, and gazed into a mirror that was brought to him. "I am old," he said; and the place was named "The old Quauhtitlan." Resting again at another place along the way, and looking back in the di-rection of his Tollan, he wept, and his tears went through a rock. He left in that place the mark of his sitting and the impress of his palms. He was met and challenged, further along, by a group of necromancers, who prohibited him from proceeding until he had left with them the knowledge of working silver, wood, and feathers, and the art of painting. As he crossed the mountains, all of his attendants, who were dwarfs and humpbacks, died of cold. At another place he encountered his antagonist, Tezcatlipoca, who defeated him at a game of ball. At still another he aimed with an arrow at a large *póchotl* tree; the arrow too was an entire *póchotl* tree; so that when he shot it through the first they formed a cross. And so he passed along, leaving many signs and place-names behind him, until, coming at last to the sea, he departed on a raft of serpents. It is not known how he arrived at his des-tination, Tlapállan, his original home.[32]

Or, according to another tradition, at the shore he immo-lated himself upon a funeral pyre, and birds with multicol-ored feathers arose from his ashes. His soul became the Morning Star.[33]

The life-eager hero can resist death, and postpone his fate for a certain time. It is written that Cuchulainn in his sleep heard a cry, "so terrible and fearful, that he fell out of his bed upon the ground, like a sack, in the east wing of the house." He rushed forth without weapons, followed by Emer, his wife, who carried his arms and garments. And he discovered a chariot harnessed with a chestnut horse that had but one leg, the pole passing through its body and out at the forehead. Within sat a woman, her eyebrows red, and a crimson mantel round her. A very big man walked along beside, also in a coat of crimson, carrying a forked staff of hazelwood and driving a cow.

Cuchulainn claimed the cow as his own, the woman challenged him, and Cuchulainn then demanded to know why she was speaking instead of the big man. She answered that the man was Uar-gaeth-sceo Luachair-sceo. "Well to be sure," said Cuchulainn, "the length of the name is astonishing!" "The woman to whom you speak," said the big man, "is called Faebor beg-beoil cuimdiuir folt sceub-gairit sceo uath." "You are making a fool of me," said Cuchulainn; and he made a leap into the chariot, put his two feet on her two shoulders, and his spear on the parting of her hair. "Do not play your sharp weapons on me!" she said. "Then tell me your true name," said Cuchulainn. "Go further off from me then," said she; "I am a female satirist, and I carry off this cow as a reward for a poem." "Let us hear your poem," said Cuchulainn. "Only move further off," said the woman; "your shaking over my head will not influence me."

Cuchulainn moved off until he was between the two wheels of the chariot. The woman sang at him a song of challenge and insult. He prepared to spring again, but, in an instant, horse, woman, chariot, man, and cow had disappeared, and on the branch of a tree was a black bird.

"A dangerous enchanted woman you are!" said Cuchulainn to the black bird; for he now realized that she was the battle-goddess, Badb, or Morrigan. "If I had only known that it was you, we should not have parted thus." "What you have done," replied the bird, "will bring you ill luck." "You cannot harm me," said Cuchulainn. "Certainly I can," said the woman; "I am guarding your deathbed, and I shall be guarding it henceforth."

Then the enchantress told him that she was taking the cow from the fairy hill of Cruachan to be bred by the bull of the big man, who was Cuailgne; and when her calf was a year old

Cuchulainn would die. She herself would come against him when he would be engaged at a certain ford with a man "as strong, as victorious, as dexterous, as terrible, as untiring, as noble, as brave, as great" as himself. "I will become an eel," she said, "and I will throw a noose round thy feet in the ford." Cuchulainn exchanged threats with her, and she disappeared into the ground. But the following year, at the foretold foray at the ford, he overcame her, and actually lived to die another day.[34]

A curious, perhaps playful, echo of the symbolism of salvation in a yonder world dimly sounds in the final passage of the Pueblo folk tale of Water Jar boy. "A lot of people were living down inside the spring, women and girls. They all ran to the boy and put their arms around him because they were glad their child had come to their house. Thus the boy found his father and his aunts, too. Well, the boy stayed there one night and next day he went back home and told his mother he had found his father. Then his mother got sick and died. Then the boy said to himself, 'No use for me to live with these people.' So he left them and went to the spring. And there was his mother. That was the way he and his mother went to live with his father. His father was Avaiyo' pi'i (water snake red). He said he could not live with them over at Sikyat'ki. That was the reason he made the boy's mother sick so she died and 'came over here to live with me,' said his father. 'Now we will live here together,' said Avaiyo' to his son. That's the way that boy and his mother went to the spring to live there." [35]

This story, like that of the clam wife, repeats point for point the mythical narrative. The two stories are charming in their apparent innocence of their power. At the opposite extreme is the account of the death of the Buddha: humorous, like all great myth, but conscious to the last degree.

"The Blessed One, accompanied by a large congregation of priests, drew near to the further bank of the Hirannavati river, and to the city of Kusinara and the sal-tree grove Upavattana of the Mallas; and having drawn near, he addressed the venerable Ananda:

" 'Be so good, Ananda, as to spread me a couch with its

head to the north between twin sal-trees. I am weary, Ananda, and wish to lie down.'

" 'Yes, Reverend Sir,' said the venerable Ananda to The Blessed One in assent, and spread the couch with its head to the north between twin sal-trees. Then The Blessed One lay down on his right side after the manner of a lion, and placing foot on foot, remained mindful and conscious.

"Now at that time the twin sal-trees had completely burst forth into bloom, though it was not the flowering season; and the blossoms scattered themselves over the body of The Tathagata, and strewed and sprinkled themselves in worship of The Tathagata.[36] Also heavenly sandal-wood powder fell from the sky; and this scattered itself over the body of The Tathagata, and strewed and sprinkled itself in worship of The Tathagata. And music sounded in the sky in worship of The Tathagata, and heavenly choruses were heard to sing in worship of The Tathagata."

During the conversations which then took place, as The Tathagata lay like a lion on his side, a large priest, the venerable Upavana, stood in front, fanning him. The Blessed One briefly ordered him to step aside; whereupon the body attendant of The Blessed One, Ananda, complained to The Blessed One. "Reverend Sir," he said, "what, pray, was the reason, and what was the cause, that The Blessed One was harsh to the venerable Upavana, saying, 'Step aside, O priest; stand not in front of me'?"

The Blessed One replied: "Ananda, almost all the deities throughout ten worlds have come together to behold The Tathagata. For an extent, Ananda, of twelve leagues about the city Kusinara and the sal-tree grove Upavattana of the Mallas, there is not a spot of ground large enough to stick the point of a hair into, that is not pervaded by powerful deities. And these deities, Ananda, are angered, saying, 'From afar have we come to behold The Tathagata, for but seldom, and on rare occasions, does a Tathagata, a saint, and Supreme Buddha arise in the world; and now, to-night, in the last watch, will The Tathagata pass into Nirvana; but this powerful priest stands in front of The Blessed One, concealing him, and we have no chance to see The Tathagata, although his last moments are near.' Thus Ananda, are these deities angered."

"What are the deities doing, Reverend Sir, whom The Blessed One perceives?"

"Some of the deities, Ananda, are in the air with their minds engrossed by earthly things, and they let fly their hair and cry aloud, and stretch out their arms and cry aloud, and fall headlong to the ground and roll to and fro, saying, 'All too soon will The Blessed One pass into Nirvana; all too soon will The Light of The World vanish from sight!' Some of the deities, Ananda, are on the earth with their minds engrossed by earthly things, and they let fly their hair and cry aloud, and stretch out their arms and cry aloud, and fall headlong on the ground and roll to and fro, saying, 'All too soon will The Blessed One pass into Nivana; all too soon will The Happy One pass into Nivana; all too soon will The Light of The World vanish from sight.' But those deities which are free from passion, mindful and conscious, bear it patiently, saying, 'Transitory are all things. How is it possible that whatever has been born, has come into being, and is organized and perishable, should not perish? That condition is not possible.' "

The last conversations continued for some time, and during the course of them The Blessed One gave consolation to his priests. Then he addressed them:

"And now, O priests, I take my leave of you; all the constituents of being are transitory; work out your salvation with diligence."

And this was the last word of The Tathagata.

"Thereupon The Blessed One entered the first trance; and rising from the first trance, he entered the second trance; and rising from the second trance, he entered the third trance; and rising from the third trance, he entered the fourth trance; and rising from the fourth trance, he entered the realm of the infinity of space; and rising from the realm of the infinity of space, he entered the realm of the infinity of consciousness, and rising from the realm of the infinity of consciousness, he entered the realm of nothingness; and rising from the realm of nothingness, he entered the realm of neither perception nor yet non-perception; and rising from the realm of neither perception nor yet non-perception, he arrived at the cessation of perception and sensation.

"Thereupon the venerable Ananda spoke to the venerable Anuruddha as follows:

" 'Reverend Anuruddha, The Blessed One has passed into Nirvana.'

" 'Nay, brother Ananda, The Blessed One has not yet passed into Nirvana; he has arrived at the cessation of perception and sensation.'

"Thereupon The Blessed One rising from the cessation of his perception and sensation, entered the realm of neither perception nor yet non-perception; and rising from the realm of neither perception nor yet non-perception, he entered the realm of nothingness; and rising from the realm of nothingness, he entered the realm of infinity of consciousness; and rising from the realm of infinity of consciousness, he entered the realm of the infinity of space; and rising from the realm of the infinity of space, he entered the fourth trance; and rising from the fourth trance, he entered the third trance; and rising from the third trance, he entered the second trance; and rising from the second trance, he entered the first trance; and rising from the first trance, he entered the second trance; and rising from the second trance, he entered the third trance; and rising from the third trance, he entered the fourth trance; and rising from the fourth trance, immediately The Blessed One passed into Nirvana." [37]

NOTES

[1] Herbert A. Giles, *A Chinese Biographical Dictionary* (London and Shanghai, 1898), pp. 233-234; Rev. J. MacGowan, *The Imperial History of China* (Shanghai, 1906), pp. 4-5; Friedrich Hirth, *The Ancient History of China* (Columbia University Press, 1908), pp. 8-9.

[2] Giles, *op. cit.,* p. 656; MacGowan, *op. cit.,* pp. 5-6; Hirth, *op. cit.,* pp. 10-12.

[3] Giles, *op. cit.,* p. 338; MacGowan, *op. cit.,* pp. 6-8; Edouard Chavannes, *Les mémoires historiques de Se-ma Ts'ien* (Paris, 1895-1905), Vol. I, pp. 25-36. See also John C. Ferguson, *Chinese Mythology* ("The Mythology of All Races," Vol. VIII, Boston, 1928), pp. 27-28, 29-31.

[4] This formula is, of course, not precisely that of the common Christian teaching, where, though Jesus is reported to have declared that "the kingdom of God is within you," the churches maintain that,

since man is created only "in the image" of God, the distinction between the soul and its creator is absolute—thus retaining, as the final reach of their wisdom, the dualistic distinction between man's "eternal soul" and the divinity. The transcending of this pair of opposites is not encouraged (indeed, is rejected as "pantheism" and has sometimes been rewarded with the stake); nevertheless, the prayers and diaries of the Christian mystics abound in ecstatic descriptions of the unitive, soul-shattering experience while Dante's vision at the conclusion of the Divine Comedy certainly goes beyond the orthodox, dualistic, concretistic dogma of the finality of the personalities of the Trinity. Where this dogma is not transcended the myth of Going to the Father is taken literally, as describing man's final goal.

As for the problem of imitating Jesus as a human model, or meditating upon Him as a god, the history of the Christian attitude may be roughly summarized, as follows: (1) a period of literally following the master, Jesus, by renouncing the world as he did (Primitive Christianity); (2) a period of meditating on Christ Crucified as the divinity within the heart, meanwhile leading one's life in the world as the servant of this god (Early and Medieval Christianity); (3) a rejection of most of the instruments supporting meditation, meanwhile, however, continuing to lead one's life in the world as the servant or vehicle of the god whom one has ceased to visualize (Protestant Christianity); (4) an attempt to interpret Jesus as a model human being, but without accepting his ascetic path (Liberal Christianity).

5 These three legends appear in the excellent psychological study by Dr. Otto Rank, *The Myth of the Birth of the Hero* (Nervous and Mental Disease Monographs; New York, 1910). A variant of the third appears in the *Gesta Romanorum,* Tale LXXXI.

6 Actually Charles the Great was beardless and bald.

7 The Charlemagne cycles are exhaustively discussed by Joseph Bédier, *Les légendes épiques* (3rd edition; Paris, 1926).

8 Louis Ginzberg, *The Legends of the Jews* (Philadelphia: The Jewish Publication Society of America, 1911), Vol. III, pp. 90-94.

9 George Bird Grinnell, *Blackfoot Lodge Tales* (New York: Charles Scribner's Sons, 1892, 1916), pp. 31-32.

10 Elsie Clews Parsons, *Tewa Tales* (Memoirs of the American Folklore Society, XIX, 1926), p. 193.

11 The sense of this advice, which to the Western reader may seem strange, is that the Way of Devotion *(bhakti mārga)* must begin with things known and loved by the devotee, not remote, unimaginable conceptions. Since the Godhead is immanent in all, He will make Himself known through any object profoundly regarded. Furthermore, it is the Godhead within the devotee that makes it possible for him to discover Godhead in the world without. This mystery is illustrated in Krishna's double presence during the act of worship.

[12] Adapted from Sister Nivedita and Ananda K. Coomaraswamy, *Myths of the Hindus and Buddhists* (New York: Henry Holt and Company, 1914), pp. 221-232.

[13] Parsons, *op. cit.*, p. 193.

[14] The legendary cycles of medieval Ireland include: *(1) The Mythological Cycle,* which describes the migrations to the island of prehistoric peoples, their battles, and in particular the deeds of the race of gods known as the Tuatha De Danaan, "Children of the Great Mother, Dana"; *(2) The Annals of the Milesians,* or semi-historical chronicles of the last arriving race, the sons of Milesius, founders of the Celtic dynasties that survived until the arrival of the Anglo-Normans under Henry II in the twelfth century; *(3) The Ulster Cycle of the Knights of the Red Branch,* which treats primarily of the deeds of Cuchulainn (pronounced coohoolinn) at the court of his uncle Conchobar (pronounced conohoor): this cycle greatly influenced the development of the Arthurian tradition, in Wales, Brittany, and England—the court of Conchobar serving as model for that of King Arthur and the deeds of Cuchulainn for those of Arthur's nephew, Sir Gawain (Gawain was the original hero of many of the adventures later assigned to Lancelot, Perceval, and Galahad); *(4) The Cycle of the Fianna:* the Fianna were a company of heroic fighters under the captaincy of Finn MacCool (cf. note, p. 223, *supra*); the greatest tale of this cycle being that of the love triangle of Finn, Grianni his bride, and Diarmaid his nephew, many episodes of which come down to us in the celebrated tale of Tristan and Iseult; *(5) Legends of the Irish Saints.*

The "little people" of the popular fairy lore of Christian Ireland are reductions of the earlier pagan divinities, the Tuatha De Danaan.

[15] "Taín bó Cuailgne" (from the version in the *Book of Leinster,* 62 a-b): edited by Wh. Stokes and E. Windisch, *Irische Texte* (Extraband zu Serie I bis IV; Leipzig, 1905), pp. 106-117; English translation in Eleanor Hull's *The Cuchullin Saga in Irish Literature* (London, 1898), pp. 135-137.

[16] *Book of Leinster,* 64B-67B (Stokes and Windisch, *op. cit.,* pp. 130-169); Hull, *op. cit.,* pp. 142-154.

[17] From Eleanor Hull, *op. cit.,* p. 154; translated from the *Book of Leinster,* 68A (Stokes and Windisch, *op. cit.,* pp. 168-171).

[18] Hull, *op. cit.,* pp. 174-176; from the *Book of Leinster,* 77 (Stokes and Windisch, *op. cit.,* pp. 368-377).

[19] Uno Holmberg (Uno Harva), *Der Baum des Lebens* (Annales Academiae Scientiarum Fennicae, Ser. B, Tom. XVI, No. 3; Helsinki, 1923), pp. 57-59; from N. Gorochov, "Yryn Uolan" *(Izvestia Vostočno-Siberskago Otdela I. Russkago Geografičeskago Obščestva,* XV), pp. 43 ff.

[20] *Kalevala,* III, 295-300; from the translation by W. F. Kirby (Everyman's Library, Nos. 259-260).

[21] I am here keeping the distinction between the earlier semi-animal

titan-hero (city founder, culture giver) and the later, fully human type. The deeds of the latter frequently include the slaying of the former, the Pythons and Minotaurs who were the boon-givers of the past. (A god outgrown becomes immediately a life-destroying demon. The form has to be broken and the energies released.) Not infrequently deeds that belong to the earlier stages of the cycle are assigned to the human hero, or one of the earlier heroes may be humanized and carried on into a later day; but such contaminations and variations do not alter the general formula.

22 Clark Wissler and D. C. Duvall, *Mythology of the Blackfeet Indians* (Anthropological papers of the American Museum of Natural History, Vol. II, Part I; New York, 1909), pp. 55-57.

23 Jacobus de Voragine, *The Golden Legend,* CIV, "St. Martha, Virgin."

24 One of a class of priests entrusted with the preparation and application of the sacred ointments.

25 Chief priest, governing as viceregent of the god.

26 Morris Edward Opler, *Myths and Tales of the Jicarilla Apache Indians* (Memoirs of the American Folklore Society, Vol. XXXI, 1938), pp. 133-134.

27 Adapted from Nivedita and Coomaraswamy, *op. cit.,* pp. 236-237.

28 Ananda K. Coomaraswamy, *Hinduism and Buddhism* (New York, The Philosophical Library, no date), pp. 6-7.

29 Matthew, 10:34-37.

30 Ginzberg, *op. cit.,* Vol. I, pp. 305-306. By permission of the Jewish Publication Society of America.

31 Wilhelm Stekel, *Die Sprache des Traumes,* dream no. 421. Death here appears, observes Dr. Stekel, in four symbols: the Old Fiddler, the Squinting One, the Old Woman, and the Young Peasant (the Peasant is the Sower and the Reaper).

32 Bernardino de Sahagún, *Historia General de las Cosas de Nueva España* (Mexico, 1829), Lib. III, Cap. xii-xiv (condensed). The work has been republished by Pedro Robredo (Mexico, 1938), Vol. I, pp. 278-282.

33 Thomas A. Joyce, *Mexican Archaeology* (London, 1914), p. 46.

34 "Taín bó Regamna," edited by Stokes and Windisch, *Irische Texte* (zweite Serie, Heft. 2; Leipzig, 1887), pp. 241-254. The above is condensed from Hull, *op. cit.,* pp. 103-107.

35 Parsons, *op. cit.,* pp. 194-195.

36 Tathāgata: "arrived at or being in *(gata)* such a state or condition *(tathā)*": i.e., an Enlightened One, a Buddha.

37 Reprinted by permission of the publishers from Henry Clarke Warren, *Buddhism in Translations* (Harvard Oriental Series, 3), Cambridge, Mass.: Harvard University Press, 1896, pp. 95-110.

SUGGESTIONS FOR DISCUSSION

1. Dorson offers some strictures on Campbell's method of interpreting myths. Do you find examples in the foregoing selection of the sort

of interpretation Dorson objects to? How would you characterize Campbell's approach to myth more fully?

2. Apply Murray's analysis of the content of myths to the childhood of the hero, as Campbell describes it. What mythic elements are present, and what absent, from this "monomyth"?

3. The hero's assault on the tyrant implies a certain attitude toward past and present. How does this attitude differ from the one which underlies the Paradise myth (as Eliade describes it)? How does the shaman's role differ from that of Campbell's hero? Can you see any way to reconcile these elements of the two mythic clusters?

4. What justification does there seem to be for treating the hero as champion of "things becoming," of change? To judge from the stories Campbell tells, could the hero as easily stand for wisdom? For virtue? For life? In other words, how much arbitrariness, if any, is there in Campbell's method of interpretation?

5. Dorson makes a distinction between sacred myths and hero sagas, but Campbell lumps them together. What differences between the two scholars' approaches to myth might explain this difference in classification?

6. What psychic ends are served by the myth of the hero as Campbell analyzes it?

THE THREE ROMES

THE MIGRATION OF AN

IDEOLOGY AND THE MAKING

OF AN AUTOCRAT

ROBERT LEE WOLFF

I

In recent years the Western world has given increasing attention [1] to the ideas expressed in a passage taken from a letter written by an early sixteenth-century Russian church-man, Philotheus (or Filofey) of Pskov, to Tsar Vassily III (reigned 1505-1534). An approximate translation reads thus:

The church of the Old Rome fell because of the Apollinarian heresy; the gates of the church of the Second Rome, Constanti-nople, have been hewn down by the axes of the infidel Turks; but

ROBERT LEE WOLFF, born in New York City in 1915, is professor of his-tory at Harvard University and is a member of the Executive Com-mittee of its Russian Research Center, of the Board of Scholars of its Dumbarton Oaks Research Library and Collection, and of the Execu-tive Committee of the Council of the Mediaeval Academy of America. During World War II he served as Chief of the Balkan Section, Re-search and Analysis Branch, Office of Strategic Services. His writings include *The Balkans in Our Time* and numerous monographic studies on medieval subjects.

the present church of the Third, New Rome, of thy sovereign Empire . . . shines in the universe more resplendent than the sun. . . . All the empires of the Orthodox Christian Faith have come together in thy single Empire. Thou are the sole Emperor of all the Christians in the whole universe. . . . For two Romes have fallen, but the Third stands, and a Fourth shall never be.[2]

Arnold Toynbee uses this passage in his essay, "Russia's Byzantine Heritage," to illustrate and demonstrate the persistence in Russia of two features that he singles out as characteristic of the Byzantine empire: a conviction of complete rightness in controversy, and a messianic sense of manifest destiny.[3] Some have embraced and embroidered the thesis, and others have challenged and ridiculed it. Those who would like a single simple explanation of the difficulties between the West and the U.S.S.R. have perhaps seized on it too eagerly. Those who are skeptical as to the importance of ideology, who doubt the continuity of ideology over the watershed of the Russian Revolution, or who are concerned with defending *Russia* as such and with attributing to communism alone the problems that face us, have perhaps dismissed it too swiftly. Whether attacked or defended, however, the idea has caught on and penetrated, usually without much preliminary reflection, into the consciousness of many Americans. Thus, Wallace Stevens wrote in 1947: *

> Say this to Pravda, tell the damned rag
> That the peaches are slowly ripening,
> Say that the American moon comes up
> Cleansed clean of lousy Byzantium.

The following remarks are intended as a gloss on the passage from Philotheus of Pskov. What is its ideology? Whence derived? And what has been the relationship of that ideology to Russian political behavior? In trying to answer the last question, I have assumed that men often adopt an ideology in order to justify some course of action already undertaken or planned, and that thereafter the political practitioner may become the victim of his own ideology. If it has been gen-

---

* Reprinted from "Memorandum" (*Opus Posthumous,* p. 89) by Wallace Stevens by permission of Alfred A. Knopf, Inc. Copyright, 1957, by Elsie Stevens and Holly Stevens.

erally accepted, or expanded, or popularized, it may seize hold of him and force him to act in a way no longer advisable for other reasons. For example, Mussolini's ideology of *Mare Nostrum,* of a revived Roman empire in the Mediterranean, served in the beginning as a nationalist spur to rebuild seaports, to create a merchant fleet and a navy; and it caused him to embark on the African and Albanian adventures—all projects he had long contemplated. But after the Fascists had spread through all available channels the idea that they were "Romans," they had to act as they themselves had insisted Romans must act: they had to move toward Mediterranean revisionism (Corsica, Nice, Tunisia, Savoy) and toward Hitler, and away from the Western democracies and the preservation of the status quo, where their interests actually lay. Political theory and political action are difficult to disentangle; but surely, if practice initially gives birth to theory, then theory in turn may eventually dictate practice.

We may immediately identify the passage from Philotheus as another example of the mystic and somehow satisfying pronouncements about the third member of a series: the churches of Rome, Constantinople, and Moscow. The churches of two of these have fallen, but that of the third stands fast: there can be no fourth. It was perhaps Joachim of Fiore (1145-1202), a Calabrian monk, who was most responsible for popularizing this way of thinking in triads. His third age of the universe, the age of the third member of the Trinity, would find its revelation in a third Testament, as the first two ages had been respectively that of the Father and the Old Testament, and that of the Son and the New. Recent students of the astonishing impact of Joachite influence on the European mind have instanced, as late reappearances of the same fantasy, the Comteian idea of history as moving successively through theological, metaphysical, and scientific phases; the Hegelian process of thesis, antithesis, and synthesis; the Marxian dialectic of primitive communism, class society, and final communism, in which the state will wither away; and even Hitler's Third Reich, whose title was invented by the nationalist Moeller van den Bruck as early as 1923, but was taken over by the Nazis because they sensed that it retained the age-old emotional impact of the third and

final member of a triad.⁴ One need not for a moment argue
that Philotheus of Pskov had read Joachim of Fiore, but only
that he did not have to do so: the Joachite concept was in the
air, and the church of the Third Rome repeats the fantasy.

For the ideology of the First Rome, ruler of the world,
center of the universal power, destined to last until the end
of time, we need only turn to Virgil (*His ego nec metas rerum
nec tempora pono / Imperium sine fine dedi. . . .—Aeneid* I,
278-279); and to appreciate the extraordinary vigor of the tradition, we turn to one of the last of the pagan poets, Rutilius
Namatianus, who echoes Virgil even in the fifth century A.D.,
when the entire structure of Roman society was in fact crum-
bling before the barbarians. In Virgil's day the transformation that turned the elected Roman chief magistrate into a
deified monarch on the Hellenistic pattern had taken place.
By the fifth century, the disappearance of the emperor from
Rome left a vacuum the Popes would eventually fill by expressing the old ideas of primacy and eternity on their own
behalf.

Meanwhile, Constantine's transfer of the seat of empire to
Byzantium and his own conversion to Christianity naturally
led to a transfer and a modification of the ideology. Constantine intended Constantinople to be a second Rome. There he
founded a new senate, transplanting many ancient aristocratic
Roman families, placing *Urbs Roma, Populus Romanus,* and
the she-wolf on his coinage along with Constantinople's goddess of fortune, even seeking to find in the new capital the
ancient topographic features of the old—the seven hills, the
fourteen regions. As early as 381 A.D., the Second Ecumenical
Council, held at Constantinople, declared that the Bishop of
Constantinople ranked second only to the Bishop of Rome,
"because Constantinople is new Rome." This was reaffirmed
in 451 at the Fourth Ecumenical Council at Chalcedon, which
simultaneously extended the ecclesiastical jurisdiction of
Constantinople, though this was specifically challenged by
Pope Leo I, who strongly objected. Even St. Augustine
agreed, however, that "God permitted Constantine to found
another city like a daughter of Rome herself." Byzantine
writers regularly called their city "New Rome." Though they
were Greeks writing in Greek, they always referred to them-

selves as "Romans" *(Rhomaioi),* never as "Hellenes," which
had come to mean "pagans." Constantinople had become the
capital of a state that regarded itself as ecumenical, or universal, embracing the whole inhabited world. Again and
again throughout the centuries the writers of Constantinople
claimed that the city was stronger and more vigorous than
the old Rome. The court poet writing the epithalamium for
the wedding of Manuel I (1143-1180) to the princess of the
Holy Roman Empire, Bertha of Sulzbach, says:

> If Old Rome supplied the bride, you [i.e., Byzantium or New
> Rome] supplied the bridegroom, and since "the head of the
> woman is the man" [1 Cor. 11, 3] so are you too the head, and the
> Old Rome only a limb of yours.

And from the West the *versus Romae* lament: "Flourishing
Constantinople is called New Rome; Old Rome, thou art
falling, both walls and ways of life [*moribus et muris*]." [5]

After Constantine, the emperor is of course no longer God,
but he is the earthly reflection of the single God in heaven,
divinely ordained, and as time passes he is bound by a code of
etiquette so complicated and rigid that every waking moment
is governed by its particular protocol. Fountainhead of law
and justice, master of his subjects, who are called by a term
that literally means slaves, he needs to consult with no one,
but resides in a sacred place, set apart. Equal to the Apostles,
he presides over the councils of the Church and gives the
force of law to the decisions of the ecclesiastics. Sometimes he
even pronounces on matters of dogma *without consulting* the
opinion of the bishops. When he does so, he may fairly be
called Caesaro-papist, since he is literally acting both as Caesar
and as Pope. But even when he takes council with the bishops,
his Church remains a department of state. Seldom in the long
course of Byzantine history is an emperor successfully challenged by a patriarch, and very seldom do we find the proposition that in the West becomes a commonplace of papal
theory: that the wielder of the spiritual power, the patriarch,
should be regarded as equal to the emperor, a claim that
logically leads directly to an assertion of superiority. (The
idea did appear in the ninth-century law book called the
Epanagoge, in a passage probably written by the Patriarch

Photius, but it had little impact on Byzantine thinking or action.[6])

It is true that in practice the emperor often fails to force through policies that might offend the religious susceptibilities of the people of Constantinople; it is true that when he disobeys the divine laws the people have the sanction of revolution; it is true that the throne eventually becomes the prize in a struggle between the landed aristocrats and the imperial bureaucracy; and true that in the period just before the successful overturn of the empire by the Crusaders in 1204, the power of the central government has weakened, local anarchy prevails, and hated Western influences are penetrating everywhere. But these developments take place in the harsh world of actuality; the Byzantine theory of the state does not alter, and its ecumenical claims are put forward with the same calm assurance during the two centuries after the Greeks have recaptured their capital in 1261 and while their empire is in fact little more than another Balkan state.

It is little wonder, perhaps, that in the period of Byzantine greatness the image of the Byzantine state should have exerted a compelling attraction on all the barbarian peoples; it is startling that the image lost little of its power even after the reality had faded, and that Bulgarians, Serbs, and Russians were held as spellbound by it in the fourteenth and fifteenth centuries as they and others had been five hundred years earlier.

Between the Second Rome and the First the sources of disagreement were many. In their desperate efforts to solve the theological controversies of the first Christian centuries—controversies in which expressions of views contrary to those put forward in Constantinople thinly veiled the national hatred of the restless Egyptians or Syrians for their Greek rulers—the Byzantine emperors often encountered grave opposition from the Popes, who did not understand (or, in some cases, want to understand) the imperial political problems in the East. So the scism over Zeno's efforts to appease the Monophysites in the last quarter of the fifth century was followed by the troubles over Justinian's attempt to legislate on dogma in the middle of the sixth century, and by renewed hostility over Heraclius' last efforts before the Arab conquests in the

seventh century. And when the image-breakers put their candidates on the throne in the eighth century, and the Popes
opposed their views, the emperors subtracted southern Italy
and Illyricum, with their rich revenues, from papal jurisdiction, and gave the quarrel between the First Rome and the
Second real political and economic content.

To these issues was added, in time, the growing discovery,
easily exploited for purposes of propaganda, that different
practices had grown up in the Eastern and Western churches.
So in the ninth century for the first time it became a burning
issue that the Latin church of the West had "added" to the
creed the word *filioque*, "and from the Son," with reference
to the procession of the Holy Ghost, who in the Greek church
proceeds from the Father only. These issues, some major,
some minor, multiplied until in 1054 one of the periodic controversies over them culminated in a break that proved permanent. Among the issues was that of the azymes: the West
used unleavened bread for the communion wafer, the East
leavened bread. The Greeks argued that the yeast in the
leaven of their communion bread symbolized the human nature that the Word of God had assumed when taking flesh. To
use unleavened bread was to deny the human nature of
Christ. This was the heresy of Apollinaris of Laodicea, and
the Roman church was guilty of it. And this is what Philotheus meant when he said that the church of the Old Rome
"fell because of the Apollinarian heresy." Actually, of course,
the church of Old Rome had not fallen, nor has it fallen yet;
but it was convenient for Philotheus' argument to assert that
it had.

II

At the end of the tenth century, the Prince of Kiev, Vladimir,
accepted Christianity from Byzantium. The Kievan princes
were members of a group of Scandinavian origin, ruling over
a Slavic population. They shared with the Germans the tradition of the war-band, Tactius' old *comitatus*, the *Gefolge*—
in Russian, *druzhina*. The members of the war-band had the
traditional right to be consulted on major questions, and they
also enjoyed the celebrated right of departure to serve some
other prince whenever they were sufficiently discontented.

Nothing could be more unlike the pattern of Byzantine autocracy. Despite the important cultural influences that entered Russia with Christianity and imbued the new church with Byzantine traditions, Kiev did not borrow extensively from the Byzantine imperial ideology; indeed, its dynastic ties were largely Western. Only toward the very end of the Kievan state, in the last quarter of the twelfth century, do we find in literature the first traces of this borrowing: one of the Russian chronicle texts takes over a passage about the good prince from a rather pedestrian and conventional sixth-century Byzantine work by Agapetus on the proper character of a ruler.[7]

So it is not until a much later period, after the collapse of the Kievan state, under pressure from outside forces and as the result of internal fragmentation, and after the long years of Tatar domination, during which much of Russia was largely cut off from Western influences, that we find emerging in the princes of Moscow the dynasty to which both the political theory of the heritage of Rome and the political practice of the Byzantine autocrat would make their appeal. First as agents of the Tatar khan, the princes of Moscow profited by the connection to assess Tatar weaknesses; then they emerged as national champions against the Tatars: a grasping, able line of princes who established the principle of primogeniture, expanded their territorial holdings, and consolidated their power.

Watching this process, the Russian church singled out the princes of Moscow as its most promising allies. In 1326 the Metropolitan chose Moscow as his official residence, and advised the Prince that if he would build a church of the Virgin and bury him in that church, the city would become celebrated above all other Russian cities, and that its resident bishops would help him defeat his enemies. A few years later, in 1339, the scribe of a manuscript of the Gospels was already comparing the prince of Moscow to the Byzantine emperors Constantine, Justinian, and Manuel Commenus: the Russian church was beginning to seek in the only tradition it knew, that of Byzantium, for precedents to make great the prince whom it had decided to support and on whom its own future depended. More and more the complexion of the church itself was becoming Russian; after the Tatar invasions the Metropolitan was more and more frequently a native Russian; direct communication with Byzantium had ceased to be easy, for during the fourteenth century the Byzantines themselves were beset by the Turks.

In 1393 we find the Patriarch of Constantinople himself complaining to the Prince of Moscow that the Russians pay insufficient honor to the Byzantine Emperor:

> Once more with grief I have heard that your highness has said certain things about the Emperor in derogation. . . . That is bad. The Emperor is not like local and provincial rulers and sovereigns. The Emperors convoked the ecumenical councils; by their own laws they sanctioned what the divine canons said about the correct dogmas and the ordering of the Christian life; they determined by their decrees the order of the episcopal sees and set up their boundaries. The church ordained the Emperor, anointed him, and consecrated him Emperor and Autocrat of all the Romans, that is, of all Christians. My most exalted and holy autocrat is by the grace of God the eternal and orthodox defender and avenger of the church. It is not possible for Christians to have a church and not to have an Emperor.[8]

This lesson in Byzantine political theory did not inspire the Russians to render fuller obedience to distant Constantinople, itself now nearly powerless. But the lesson was not lost: the ambitious Muscovite church and state were learning what it was to be absolute.

So long as the Byzantine Empire lasted, the Second Rome was in being, and Moscow could hardly claim to have superseded it. Two crucial events of the fifteenth century, however, made possible the development of the complete ideology. At the Council of Ferrara-Florence, in 1439, the representatives of the Byzantine Empire, now under intolerable pressure from the Turks, agreed to a new union with Rome, officially ending the schism. They did this, of course, with the utmost reluctance, in the hope of obtaining from the West sufficient help against the enemy. As in the case of the other official attempts at reunion with the Roman church, Byzantine public opinion repudiated it. Although the Russian representatives at the council, the Greek Isidore of Kiev, accepted the union, he was repudiated too. In 1441 Tsar Vassily II ousted him, declaring that the old faith had been altered by the agreement with Rome, and that the dreadful teachings of the *filioque* and the unleavened bread must not be allowed to corrupt the faith.[9] The ouster of Isidore virtually put the Russian church and empire out of communion with Constantinople, which now stood charged with dealing with schismatics. Only a dozen years later, in 1453, came the vengeance of the Lord some Russians had been predicting: the Turks took Constantinople and put an end to the Byzantine Empire. The Second Rome had disappeared: the gates had been hewn down by the infidel Turks, the Byzantines had been punished for their agreement with Rome. It was also clear who must be their successors.

In Russia, as everywhere else in the Christian world, the fall of Constantinople made a deep impression. A certain Nestor, a Russian who had been converted to Islam and was actually present in the Turkish armies outside the city, reported that during the siege he had seen a great flame burst from the dome of Saint Sophia and rise up into the air: this was proof that the grace of God had abandoned Byzantium. Fables figuring the eventual victory of Christianity over Islam circulated widely, despite the temporary triumph of the Muslims; prophecies were rife, and one effort to interpret obscure passages in Ezekiel even led to a prediction that it was the Russians who were destined to rescue Constantinople in the end, after 365 years of bondage.[10] Though these ideas may not have had much practical effect at the time (there was no thought, for example, of a Russian attack on the formidable Ottoman Turks), the Russian church at least as early as 1461 echoed the old Byzantine political theory of the emperor in its description of Vassily II as

the man chosen by God, beloved by God, respected by God, enlightened by God, and sent by God, who governs you in the righteous ways of laws appointed by God, that divinely wise student of the holy law, only supporter of the true Orthodoxy, invested by God and ruling in his greatness, Vassily, crowned by God in his orthodoxy, Tsar of all Rus.[11]

Ivan III, son of this Vassily, in 1472 married Sophia (or Zoë) Palaeologina, niece of the last Byzantine emperor—a marriage curiously enough sponsored in the first instance by

by the Pope, who hoped that Sophia, as the representative of
the recently concluded union between the Greek and Latin
churches, would bring Russia over to Rome. When Sophia
set out for Russia, the Pope gave her a splendid retinue
headed by a papal legate, who wore a scarlet robe, had a
crucifix carried before him in the Roman manner, and did
not venerate the icons. As the procession approached Moscow,
the news spread that a schismatic churchman was about to
arrive. An assembly of Russian nobles was held to debate
whether to receive him; the deciding argument was provided
by the Metropolitan of Moscow:

Such honors [he said to Ivan III] may not be rendered to a legate
of the Pope. If he comes in one gate of your city of Moscow preceded by his cross, I, your spiritual father, will leave by another.[12]

Messengers set out at once, and forced the legate to abandon
his cross, Sophia herself intervening against him. Here the
homeless daughter of the conquered Second Rome, sponsored
by the splendid Renaissance prince who was Pope of the First
Rome, symbolically repudiated him and accepted the Orthodox and Byzantine principles of the nascent and still un-
avowed Third Rome—then little more than a collection of
log huts huddled together in the boundless plain, lacking the
characteristic towers and domes with which she and her husband and the Italian architects they imported would soon begin to embellish it.

Among the Byzantine sources, one most suggestive phrasing
of the feeling of superiority of the Second Rome over the
First is to be found in a twelfth-century verse chronicler, Constantine Manasses, writing, like all ancient chroniclers, a
complete history of the world since creation. When he comes
to the sack of Rome by the Vandals in 455, some 700 years
before his own day, he describes its horrors and then remarks:

This is what happened to Old Rome. Ours, however [i.e., Con-
stantinople], flourishes, thrives, is strong and young. May it continue to grow eternally, O Lord of all, since it has so great an
Emperor, whose light shines far abroad, victor in a thousand battles, Manuel, the golden glowing scarlet rose, with whose brilliance a thousand suns cannot compare.

Two centuries after it was written, the chronicle of Manasses was one of those Byzantine books translated into Slavonic in neighboring Bulgaria, at a time when Byzantium was weakening and Bulgaria was enjoying a revival. When the translator reached the passage about the sack of Rome, he yielded to the obvious temptation. The Vandal sack, he said, happened to Old Rome, but then he attributed to the Bulgarian capital, Tirnovo, and the Bulgarian Tsar, Asen Alexander, all the glory that Manasses had reserved for Constantinople and the Emperor Manuel:

This happened to Old Rome, but our new imperial city flourishes, thrives, is strong and young. It will remain so to the end of time because it is under the dominion of the high Tsar of the Bulgarians, the generous, the noble, the friend of the monk, the great Tsar, Asen Alexander, whose lordship cannot be outshone by numberless suns.

In one of the manuscripts there is even a portrait of Asen Alexander dressed in full Byzantine imperial regalia, receiving a crown from an angel. Before Bulgaria fell to the Turks in the late fourteenth century, the Manasses chronicle, as well as other literary monuments, had been transmitted direct to Russia in a new wave of that South Slavic cultural influence to which Muscovite culture and ideology owed so much. By 1512, we have it in a version in which the native Russian scribe has yielded to the temptation that beset his Bulgarian predecessor, and has ascribed to Moscow and to Ivan III the role claimed for the Byzantines by Manasses. The elements needed for the ideology expressed by Philotheus of Pskov are now all present: the political theory of the Third Rome is complete.[13] In fact, he may himself have written the words of the Russian version.

In the years after Philotheus, of course, the doctrine received a variety of elaborations and adornments, refinements and additions. Philotheus himself once represented the church as the woman of *Revelations* 12:1, "clothed with the sun and the moon under her feet and upon her head a crown of twelve stars." She had fled from Old Rome because of the heresy of the unleavened bread, but had found no peace in New Rome because its church had united with the Latins.

"But then she fled to the Third Rome, that is Moscow in new great Russia. Now she shines, the holy apostolic church, more brightly than the sun in the whole world and the great and pious Russian Tsar alone protects her." [14] In one of the cycles of popular stories, there appear the insignia of empire, originally belonging to Nebuchadnezzar of Babylon himself, and translated in a carnelian (or sardonyx) box to Byzantium, and thence by Vladimir, ancestor of the tsars of Moscow, to Kiev. Here the storyteller pushes the roots of Muscovite imperial legitimacy back into the Old Testament period, in accordance with the deep and widespread interest of the Russians in the Old Testament. In the "Legend of the Princes of Vladimir," written down in the late fifteenth century, we find the Emperor Augustus sending his entirely legendary brother Prus to the banks of the Vistula to organize that part of the world; fourteen generations later the Russians invite Prus's direct descendant Rurik to come and rule over them; and of course the Muscovite tsars are directly descended from Rurik. Here, too, material regalia—a piece of the True Cross and the Byzantine imperial crown—enter the story, as presents sent to the tsar by the Byzantine emperor, who begs to be left in peace.

The "Legend" identifies the tsar receiving the insignia as Vladimir (972-1015), adding that after he received them he took the name Monomakh, after the Byzantine Emperor Constantine Monomachus. Of course, like the rest of the account, this is pure fable: Constantine IX Monomachus (1042-1055) reigned several decades later than Vladimir, who never took the name Monomakh; while the true Vladimir Monomakh (1113-1125) reigned a half-century later still, and got his name from his Byzantine mother. Uneasy because of their own defiance of chronology, the Russian storytellers invented the additional feature that the regalia were not to be used until such time as God should send a worthy ruler to the Russians. Later still, they shifted the name of the Byzantine imperial donor to Alexius I (1081-1118), a true contemporary of Monomakh. In the sixteenth century, the Muscovite tsars began to be invested on their coronation with a short cap and jacket of Byzantine manufacture, which were declared to be the actual objects sent so many centuries earlier by Constantine Monomachus, and held in reserve until now. They were in fact used down to the coronation of Nicholas II in 1894, and were regarded as the living "proof" of the truth of the legends. Here then, in false genealogies of a kind first popularized by the South Slavs, who also claimed Augustus or Constantine the Great as ancestors of their rulers, and in regalia and myths about regalia, the church disseminated the fictions that helped establish the Tsar. On the one hand, the Prus legend is solemnly cited as historic fact in a treaty with the Poles; on the other, popular ballads proclaim about the tsar (in this case, Ivan the Terrible, 1534-1584): "I brought the regalia from Tsargrad [Constantinople],/Put on the imperial purple,/ Took the mace of Empire in hand./I shall drive the traitors out of Moscow." [15] So the ideology penetrated into the popular consciousness at all levels of sophistication.

Nor did the church neglect itself. Simultaneously it went back to an old and spurious claim, originally invented by the Byzantines for the church of Constantinople, that the Apostle Andrew, the first-called, the elder brother of Peter, who had introduced Peter to Our Lord, had undertaken a mission to the Scythians. He had blessed the site where Kiev would rise, and had declared that this Russian land would in the far-distant future maintain the true faith. So the churchmen provided for their own institution a direct claim to apostolic foundation, and that by Peter's *elder* brother.[16] What more could one ask for the center of orthodoxy, the only possessor of the truth in all the world?

III

It remains to suggest some of the ways in which the new ideology affected Russian political behavior. After Ivan III and Sophia had been married in 1472, he used the title "tsar" (almost surely derived from "Caesar"), and adopted the Byzantine double-headed eagle as the symbol of the Russian monarchy. Though actually a fairly distant relative, Sophia called herself heiress to Byzantium, and signed an embroidery "Empress of Byzantium." Like the Byzantine emperors, Ivan was crowned with imperial splendor; he made his sons co-rulers during his lifetime; he began to use the title *samoder-*

zhets, the precise equivalent of the Byzantine *autokrator,* the man who rules by himself, the autocrat. The imperial couple built the Kremlin, the Muscovite version of the Byzantine sacred palace, the residence set apart, where the emperor lived. Ivan began to isolate himself and to make decisions without consulting his nobles. He began to deny them the right to depart and serve another master. He punished them for protesting against his autocratic behavior.

So under Ivan the older Kievan Scandinavian relationship between ruler and fellow warriors was replaced by the imperial pattern suitable to the supreme master of the Chritsian world. The nobles of course objected, and went on objecting. Indeed, one of the most frequently repeated themes in Russian political life, for three centuries after Ivan III, was the noble's claim that he had a right to be consulted. When one of the leading Russian boyars, Prince Kurbsky, fled in the 1560's, from Ivan IV (the Terrible), he claimed that he was exercising the ancient right of departure, and wrote polemical pamphlets demanding that the tsar consult his nobles as a matter of right. In his response, Ivan referred to all his subjects by the word that means slaves. He strengthened his ringing affirmation of absolutism on the Byzantine pattern by opening a reign of terror against the great nobles.

In 1606, when a certain Prince Shuysky, representative of the class of the great boyars, managed to become tsar briefly during the so-called "Time of Troubles," the oligarchy whom he represented extracted from him the promise to consult with them, and not to punish them arbitrarily. Even after Peter the Great (1689-1725) had to all appearances riveted the shackles of universal state service upon all the nobility, regardless of their origin, the boyars of ancient birth emerged again after his death. In 1730 they imposed on the new Empress Anne, as a condition for her mounting the throne, a set of "articles" that revealed how little their program had changed: she promised to consult them—that is to say, a small council of great nobles—before taking any fundamental decisions. For a few brief weeks, until Anne realized that the newer military-service gentry would support her against the boyars of ancient birth, she governed according to the "articles." Then she tore them up. When Catherine the Great called her legislative commission in 1766 and the representatives of the different classes had their opportunity to put forward their views on Russian life in general, Prince Shcherbatov—far from a recactionary, indeed later a great admirer of George Washington—advanced opinions and claims in no way different from those of Prince Kurbsky two centuries earlier. Despite the repeated blows dealt to the old boyars—by Ivan IV; by the Time of Troubles, in which they were discredited as the friends of Poland; by Peter the Great, who forced them to amalgamate as a class with the upstart service gentry; and by the foreign advisers of Peter's successors—the old Kievan tradition died extremely hard.

Despite boyar objections (and, of course, there was no parallel to this in Byzantium), the autocracy, new in the fifteenth century, was even then firmly established in Russia. We find Ivan III in 1489 writing to the Austrian emperor, whose subject, Poppel, had just discovered Russia, and who had injudiciously offered to give Ivan a royal crown:

> By God's grace we have been lords in our land since the days of our earliest ancestors. God has elevated us to the same position which they held, and we beg him to grant us and our children our rulership in eternity as now. We have never wished for and do not wish for confirmation of this from any other source.[17]

When a German traveler, Herberstein, visited Moscow under Vassily III (1505-1534), Philotheus' Tsar, son of Ivan III, he commented:

> In the power which he exercises over his subjects he easily outstrips the rulers of the whole world. He makes use of his authority in spiritual as well as temporal affairs; he freely and of his own will decides concerning the lives and property of everybody; of the councilors whom he has, none is of such authority that he dares to disagree or in any way to resist. They say publicly that the will of the prince is the will of God.[18]

Ivan the Terrible's arbitrary autocratic rule hardly needs comment. And despite the anguish of the autocracy and the nation during the Time of Troubles (1605-1613) and the appearance of a kind of national assembly, the *zemsky sobor,* which tided Russia over the dynastic break and elected a new dynasty in 1613, the autocracy as such remained unchallenged. By the end of the seventeenth century, the *zemsky sobor* had disappeared.

In their relations with the church, the tsars outdid the Byzantine emperors. In 1589, when the Metropolitan of Moscow was made patriarch, the Patriarch of Constantinople himself performed the consecration, and spoke in the very words of Philotheus of Pskov:

Since the old Rome fell because of the Apollinarian heresy, and the Second Rome, which is Constantinople, is possessed by the godless Turks [the masters of the speaker himself], thy great Russian Tsardom, pious Tsar . . . is the Third Rome . . . and thou alone under heaven art called the Christian Tsar in the whole world for all Christians; and therefore this very act of establishing the Patriarchate will be accomplished according to God's will. . . .

Even the exceptions prove the rule. Twice in the seventeenth century the tsar granted the patriarch the title of "Great Sovereign," together with major political responsibilities. But the episodes came about almost by accident. In the first case, the patriarch actually was the tsar's own father, and had almost been elected to the throne some fifteen years before his son. In the second case, Tsar Alexis Romanov (1645-1676) admired and trusted his Patriarch Nikon. But Nikon had read the wrong Byzantine book, the *Epanagoge*, with its introduction by Photius, which led him to claim temporal as well as spiritual supremacy over the tsar, actually quoting Photius' own words written eight centuries earlier.

This sounded the unmistakable danger signal. Not only was Nikon deposed—thus proving dramatically that the power remained in the hands of the tsar—but Tsar Alexis Romanov's own son, Peter the Great, eventually (1721) went so far as to abolish the Patriarchate as an institution, declaring that he did so in order that no second Nikon might ever arise to make such claims again:

For the common people [says Peter's decree] do not understand the difference between the spiritual power and that of the autocrat; but, dazzled by the splendor and glory of the highest pastor, they think he is a second sovereign of like power with the autocrat or even more, and that the spiritual post is another and better sovereignty. If then there should be any difference of opinion between the Patriarch and the Tsar, it might easily happen that the people, perhaps misled by designing persons, should take the part of the Patriarch in the mistaken belief that they were fighting for God's cause.[19]

For the patriarch, he substituted the "clerical college" or the Holy Synod, a committee of bishops that soon came under the direction of a lay procurator. Here the principle of Caesaro-papism triumphed as it had never done at Byzantium.

I am well aware that some scholars minimize the importance of Byzantine influence in helping to shape muscovite absolutism, and point instead to the Tatar khanate, for so long the overlord of all northeast Russia, including Moscow, as supplying the model for autocracy. Nor would I exclude the importance of the Tatar precedents. Yet the weight of the evidence seems to me overwhelming that the church's doctrine of the Third Rome and its popularization of Byzantine political theory, stimulated by the Byzantine marriage of Ivan III, gave the princes of Moscow precisely the ideological assistance they needed in transforming themselves into autocrats. Indeed, much of Moscow's success in overcoming the Tatars depended precisely upon the fact that the Muscovite princes could put themselves forward as the champions of Christianity and of Russia. If it was indeed the Tatar khan on whom they were modeling themselves, can one contest the fact that Byzantine ideology enabled them to succeed? And if, as seems to me more likely, it was rather the vanished supreme master of the Christian *oikoumene,* the emperor of Rome or of Byzantium, whom they were aping, was not his political theory all the more essential to their success?

Finally, one may note the way in which the ideology of autocracy established its own tyranny: if a state rests on generally accepted assumptions, it is almost impossible to challenge those assumptions without damaging the structure of the state. As Russian history passes before us, even those tsars of the greatest good will and most liberal tendencies find themselves in a way the prisoners of Muscovite ideology. Catherine II and her grandson Alexander I play at being liberals, but neither can be sure of anything in the end except the tsars' divinely appointed mission. Catherine's admiration for Montesquieu and Beccaria and Blackstone vanishes like a puff of smoke in the first drafty current of air from the French Revolution; she toughens and becomes reactionary, murmuring something reminiscent of Herberstein about the huge size of her dominions and the unsuitability of any except an autocratic government.

Alexander's tricolor cockade, sported on the day the Bastille fell, was a young man's whim. As tsar, he and his Secret Committee of intimates, including the young Stroganov, an ex-member in good standing of the Jacobin Club of Paris, found themselves hesitant to do much except smoke cigars and drink brandy after dinner; Speransky's careful plan for subordinating the tsar to the law died aborning; it was Madame de Krüdener and Metternich who eventually prevailed over Alexander, filling him full of satisfying mysticism, manifest destiny, and legitimacy; and it was the brutal Arakcheev who in the end administered the domains of this autocrat *malgré lui*. In the last two centuries after Peter the Great, only Alexander II, under the lash of circumstances, ever made a serious attempt to modify the social and political institutions associated with autocracy, and he was assassinated before he could consolidate his work.

Meanwhile the positive supporters of autocracy were never silent. In the Slavophiles it found a kind of advocacy that even won many liberals. Repudiating as alien the "materialistic" West and all its ways, as well as Peter the Great, who had wanted to "corrupt" the purity of Russian institutions, they proclaimed the unique virtues of Byzantine Christianity, longed for a paternal and responsible autocracy that had in fact never existed, and urged a revival of the *zemsky sobor* with which the ruler might consult, instead of the creation of a parliament that might serve as a check upon him. It is arresting to turn to the works of Pobedonostsev, tutor and intellectual preceptor of the last two tsars, setting down at the turn of the twentieth century an impassioned defense of the purest theory of divinely ordained absolutism. It is fantastic to discover the Empress Alexandra, wife of Nicholas II, writing (in the English that all Victoria's grandchildren pre-

ferred) to her beloved husband at the front during the First
World War:

> . . . thank God our Emperor is an *Autocrat* . . . only you must
> show more power and decision.
>
> How they all need to feel an *iron will & hand*—it has been a
> reign of gentleness & now must be the one of power & firmness—
> you are the Lord & Master in Russia & God Almighty placed you
> there & they shall bow down before your wisdom & firmness,
> enough of kindness, wh. they were not worthy of & thought they
> could hoist you around their finger. . . . Lovy you must be
> firm. . . .
>
> You are the head & protector of the Church. . . . Show your fist,
> chastisen [sic], be the master and the lord, you are the *Autocrat* &
> they dare not forget it.
>
> . . . they are nothing and you are all, anointed by God. Be Peter
> the Great, John the Terrible, Emperor Paul—crush them all under
> you. . . .[20]

Silly though the Empress was ("now don't you laugh, noughty
[sic] one," she appends to the last injunction), these letters
(written in 1915 and 1916, while the Russian forces were
dying in their millions on the front, while the hapless and
dedicated *Duma* politicians and civil servants strove to com-
bat the corruption and intrigue that centered round her
friend Rasputin), none the less reflect her deeply felt convic-
tions—and she had enormous personal influence. On the very
eve of the Revolution of 1917, the Muscovite ideology still
flourished.

Even the masses of the Russian population, tried though
they so often were beyond bearing and to the point of revolt,
in a curious way subscribe to the ideology. So the earlier up-
risings (Bolotnikov's in 1605, Razin's in 1676, Pugachev's in
1773, to mention only three) take on the same pattern: discontented serfs combine with unruly Cossack frontiersmen;
they burn the manor houses and kill the landlords and officials. But the rebels never proclaim that the tsar must go, or
direct their forces against him. Either they maintain that the
tsar is on their side and would be horrified if he only knew
what crimes his officials and the landlords have been perpe-
trating, or their leaders announce that they *are* in fact the
tsar: false Dmitris, false Alexises, false Peter III's on their

way to join their loving Catherine, and the like. In 1825, fifty years after Pugachev, who had gone the way of the others despite his intellectual superiority and strategic ability, when the Decembrists, in accordance with the liberal principles they had learned in France, start a revolution from above, they find that they must lie to the troops and revolt in the name of the "legitimate" Tsar Constantine in Warsaw, for whom they had no more liking than for Nicholas I himself. When Muraviev-Apostol, of the southern branch of the revolutionary society, reads aloud to the peasants in a Ukrainian village a ringing denunciation of the Tsar, and declares that Christ and Christ alone can be the proper ruler, the peasants inquire in bewilderment *what* tsar it is to whom they should take their oath. And fifty years later still, in the 1870's, when the idealistic Western-oriented reformers and revolutionaries "go to the people" and dedicate themselves to the welfare of the peasantry and try to educate them as to their grievances against the tsar, the peasants turn the Populists over to the tsar's police by the hundred.

Is it too much to say that the adoption, at the end of the Tatar period and the beginning of the tsardom, of a Byzantine imperial ideology in some measure helped determine the character of the rulers' own behavior, and shaped their own and their people's attitudes toward the nature of their society and the role of the autocrat within it?

NOTES

1 The best study of the subject remains Hildegard Schaeder, *Moskau das dritte Rom* (Hamburg, 1929), Osteuropäische Studien herausgegeben vom Osteuropäischen Seminar der Hambürgischen Universität, Heft 1. The following more recent works deal more or less directly with the central problem: N. S. Chaev, " 'Moskva—Tretii Rim' v politicheskie praktike Moskovskogo Pravitel'stva XVI veka," *Istoricheskie Zapiski* 17 (1945), 3-23; G. Olšr, S.J., "Gli ultimi Rurikidi e le basi ideologiche della sovranità dello stato russo," *Orientalia Christiana Periodica* 12 (1946), 322-373; E. Denisoff, "Aux origines de l'église russe autocéphale," *Revue des Etudes Slaves* 23 (1947), 66-68; H. Rahner, *Vom ersten bis zum dritten Rom* (Innsbruck, n.d. [1950]), his inaugural address as Rector of the University of Innsbruck; O. Ogloblin, *Moskovs'ka Teoriya III Rimu v XVI-XVII stol* (Munich, 1951); W. K. Medlin, *Moscow and East Rome, A Political Study of the Relations of Church and State in Muscovite*

Russia (Geneva, 1952), Etudes d'Histoire Economique, Politique et Sociale, I; D. Strémooukhoff, "Moscow the Third Rome: Sources of the Doctrine," *Speculum* 28 (1953), 84-101; C. Toumanoff, "Moscow the Third Rome: Genesis and Significance of a Politico-Religious Idea," *The Catholic Historical Review* 40 (1955), 411-447. Chaev writes from the Soviet point of view; Olšr, Denisoff, Rahner, Strémooukhoff and Toumanoff from the Roman Catholic; and Ogloblin from the Ukrainian. I have not seen M. de Taube, "A propos de 'Moscou, troisième Rome,'" *Russie et Chrétienté* 3-4 (1948), 17-24.

2 V. Malinin, *Starets Eleazarova Monastyrya Filofei i ego Poslaniya* (Kiev, 1901), pp. 50 and 55 of the third, separately paginated, portion of the work, which gives the original Old Slavonic texts of two versions of the letter. I have substituted "infidel Turks" for the original "Agarenes" (descendants of Hagar), the usual term for Muslims at Byzantium. The quotation as given here, and as usually cited by scholars, requires a conflation of passages from the two variants of the text—a point they do not mention. I have not been able to consult the version published in *Pravoslavnyi Sobesednik* of Kazan for January, 1863. Philotheus' letters to Munekhin, official under Vassily III (see Malinin, pp. 266 ff.), still further elaborate the theme. See below.

3 First published in *Horizon,* August 1947; reprinted in *Civilization on Trial* (London, 1948), pp. 164-183. For a thoughtful challenge to Toynbee (not, however, convincing to me) see D. Obolensky, "Russia's Byzantine Heritage," *Oxford Slavonic Papers* I (1950), 37-63.

4 See, most recently, Norman Cohn, *The Pursuit of the Millennium* (Fair Lawn, N. J.: Essential Books, Inc., 1957), pp. 99 ff. and 391-392.

5 Among the very numerous recent works on Constantine, see H. Dörries, *Das Selbstzeugnis Kaiser Konstantins* (Göttingen, 1954), Abhandlungen der Akademie der Wissenchaften in Göttingen, Philosophisch-historische Klasse, Folge 3, Nr. 34; and L. Voelkl, *Der Kaiser Konstantin* (Munich, 1957); also, J. M. C. Toynbee, "Roma and Constantinopolis in Late Antique Art," *Journal of Roman Studies* 37 (1947), 135-144. Regarding the rank of the city after Rome, see A. Grillmeier and H. Bacht, eds., *Das Konzil von Chalkedon* II (Würzburg, 1953), pp. 433-562, articles by T. O. Martin, E. Herman, and A. Michel, with many references to other literature. For St. Augustine, *De civitate dei,* V, 25; the Epithalamium for Manuel I in C. Neumann, *Griechische Geschichtsschreiber und Geschichtsquellen im zwölften Jahrhundert* (Leipzig, 1888), p. 55; the *Versus Romae* most conveniently in Monumenta Germaniae Historica, *Poetae Latinae* III (Berlin, 1896), pp. 555 ff.; for discussion, W. Hammer, "The New or Second Rome in the Middle Ages," *Speculum* 19 (1944), 50-62, especially p. 53, n. 6.

[6] J. Scharf, "Photius und die Epanagoge," *Byzantinische Zeitschrift* 49 (1956), pp. 385-400, with bibliographical references.

[7] Sevčenko, "A Neglected Byzantine Source of Muscovite Ideology," *Harvard Slavic Studies* II (1954), pp. 142-179.

[8] Metropolitan Peter's advice to Ivan I in 1326 is cited from E. Golubinsky, *Istoriya Russkoi Tserkvi* (2nd edn., Moscow, 1901-1911), II, 1, p. 144; the eulogy of Ivan and the comparison with the Byzantine emperors is taken from a manuscript of Siisk by I. I. Sreznevsky, "Svedeniya i zametki o maloizvestnykh i neizvestnykh pamyatnikakh," *Zapiski Imperatorskoi Akademii Nauk* 34 (1879), *Prilozhenie,* pp. 145 ff., no. 86. For relations with Byzantium, see D. Obolensky, "Byzantium, Kiev and Moscow," *Dumbarton Oaks Papers* XI (1957), 21-78. The Patriarch's letter in the Greek text is in F. Miklošich and I. Müller, *Acta et Diplomata Graeca Medii Aevi* II (Vienna, 1862), p. 191.

[9] See especially M. Cherniavsky, "The Reception of the Council of Florence in Moscow," *Church History* 24 (1955), 347-359; and the articles by I. Sevčenko and D. Geanakoplos in the same issue of the same journal.

[10] N. K. Gudzy, *History of Early Russian Literature,* trans. Susan Wilbur Jones (New York: The Macmillan Company, 1949), pp. 258-259.

[11] A. Popov, *Istoriko-Literaturnyi Obzor Drevne-Russkykh Polemicheskikh Sochinenii protiv Latinyan* (Moscow, 1875), pp. 394-395; this book is inaccessible to me, and I cite from the review by A. Pavlov, *Otchet o Devyatnadtsatom Prisuzhdenii Nagrad Grafa Uvarova* (St. Petersburg, 1878), pp. 293-294.

[12] P. Pierling, *La Russie et le Saint-Siège* (Paris, 1896), I, p. 171.

[13] The three passages are confronted by Schaeder, *op. cit.,* p. 51, who quotes all three in the original. Strémooukhoff (*loc. cit.,* p. 86, n. 13) challenges this interpretation (but unconvincingly to me and to Toumanoff, *loc. cit.,* p. 437, n. 67).

[14] Malinin, *op. cit.,* pp. 62 ff. of texts at the end; commentary in Schaeder, p. 55, and Strémooukhoff, pp. 98-99.

[15] Gudzy, *op. cit.,* pp. 261 ff.

[16] See the splendid recent book by F. Dvornik, *The Idea of Apostolicity in Byzantium and the Legend of the Apostle Andrew* (Cambridge, Mass.: Harvard University Press, 1958), on the legend in general; on its origins in Russia, see A. Pogodin, "Povest o khozhdenii Apostola Andreya v Rusi," *Byzantino-slavica* 7 (1937-1938), 128-148.

[17] I have not seen *Pamyatniki Diplomaticheskikh Snoshenii Drevni Rossii s Derzhavami Inostrannymi,* of which Part I is "Snoshenii Knyazei Ioanna Vasilievicha i Vasilya Ioannovicha s Imperatorimi Germanskimi, 1488-1517" (St. Petersburg, 1851), so I cite this passage from F. Adelung, *Kritischliterarische Ubersicht der Reisenden in Russland* (St. Petersburg-Leipzig, 1846), I, p. 153.

[18] Sigismund, Baron Herberstein, Neyperg, and Guettenhaag, *Rerum*

Moscovitarum Commentarii (Basel, 1551), p. 17. He goes on to speculate as to whether the physical mass of the Russian nation required tyranny, or whether tyranny had rendered them hulking and cruel: "Incertum est an tanta immanitas gentis tyrannum principem exigat; an tyrannide principis gens ipsa tam immanis tamque dura crudelisque reddatur" (p. 18).

19 The Patriarch of Constantinople, in *Sobranie Gossudarstvennykh Gramot i Dogovorov* II (Moscow, 1819), p. 97, col. 2. The most recent discussion of Nikon and the *Epanagoge* is in Medlin, *op. cit.* The text of Peter's "Reglament" is in *Polnoe Sobranie Zakonov Rossiiskoi Imperii*, I, 6 (St. Petersburg, 1830), no. 3718, p. 314; see also V. M. Gribovskii, *Pamyatniki Russkago Zakonodatel'stva XVIII Stoletiya* (St. Petersburg, 1907), pp. 176 ff.

20 *The Letters of the Tsaritsa to the Tsar* 1914-1916 (London: Duckworth & Co., 1923), pp. 145, 150, 156-157, 168, 455.

SUGGESTIONS FOR DISCUSSION

1. Wolff examines the impact on history of a myth-like ideology. Consider the role of myths or fragments of myth in one of the following: the rise of Hitler; the Crusades; the career of Alexander the Great; the Spanish Inquisition; the American Civil War; the founding of Israel.

2. Are there any echoes in Soviet ideology today of the myth of the Third Rome?

3. To what extent does the idea of the third Rome qualify as a myth under Murray's definitions?

4. By what psychic process did the Tsars make use of the myth?

5. What do Wolff's findings suggest about the attitudes toward myth of men in power? In what spirit did the Russian autocrats adopt as dogma legends and spurious genealogies?

MYTH AND IDENTITY

JEROME S. BRUNER

We know now a new origin of the faint hissing of the
sea in the conch shell held to the ear. It is in part the tremor
and throb of the hand, resonating in the shell's chambers.
Yet, inescapably, it is the distant sea. For Yeats, it would have
been a reaffirmation of his proper query:

> O body swayed to music, O brightening glance,
> How can we know the dancer from the dance?

And so with myth. It is at once an external reality and the
resonance of the internal vicissitudes of man. Richard Chase's
somewhat cumbersome definition will at least get us on our
way: "Myth is an esthetic device for bringing the imaginary
but powerful world of preternatural forces into a manageable
collaboration with the objective [i.e., experienced] facts of
life in such a way as to excite a sense of reality amenable to
both the unconscious passions and the conscious mind."

That myth has such a function—to effect some manner of

JEROME S. BRUNER was born in New York in 1915. He is professor of
psychology and director of the Cognition Project at Harvard University.
He is the author of various books and articles on the nature of thought
processes and perception, several of which deal with the manner in
which myth and literature pattern man's ideas and concepts about himself and the world in which he lives. His most recent book was *A Study
of Thinking*.

harmony between the literalities of experience and the night impulses of life—few would deny any longer. Yet I would urge that we not be too easily tempted into thinking that there is an oppositional contrast between *logos* and *mythos,* the grammar of experience and the grammar of myth. For each complements the other, and it is in the light of this complementarity that I wish to examine the relation of myth and personality.

Consider the myth first as a projection, to use the conventional psychoanalytic term. I would prefer the term "externalization," for I do not refer solely to the tendency to project outward simulacra only of those impulses that we cannot accept in ourselves. We might begin, rather, with the human preference to cope with events that are outside rather than those that are inside. Freud long ago remarked on this preference, noting that in so far as we were able to do so, we converted inner stimuli into seemingly outer events as if better to protect ourselves. So it is in the dream, where impulse is transduced into image and symbol, where an internal plight is converted into a story plot. So, too, even in rather simple forms of motor learning, where, after mastery, a pattern of muscular movements is rendered into a visualized image of a path of movement. And when we are painting a picture or writing a poem or constructing a scientific theory, there comes a moment when "it," the product we are producing, takes over and develops an autonomy of its own, an external existence. It is now the theory that requires the revision, not the theorist, the picture that needs this line here, and not the painter's whim.

What is the significance of this externalizing tendency? It is twofold, I would urge. It provides, in the first instance, a basis for communion between men. What is "out there" can be named and shared in a manner beyond the sharing of subjectivity. By the subjectifying of our worlds through externalization, we are able, paradoxically enough, to share communally in the nature of internal experience. By externalizing cause and effect, for example, we may construct a common matrix of determinism. Fate, the full of the moon, the aether—these and not our unique fears are what join us in common reaction. But perhaps more important still, externalization makes possible the containment of terror and impulse by the decorum of art and symbolism. Given man's search for art forms, it must surely be no accident that there is no art of internal feeling or impulse. We seem unable to impose what Freud once called the artifice of formal beauty upon our internal sensations or even upon our stream of seemingly uncontrolled fantasy. It is in the act of fashioning an external product out of our internal impulses that the work of art begins. There is no art of kinesthesis, and for all Huxley's fantasies, there will not be an art of the "feelies." Sharing, then, and the containment of impulse in beauty— these are the possibilities offered by externalization.

Let me illustrate my point by reference to Sophocles, particularly to the madness of Ajax. Recall the occasion of the death of Achilles and the determination of Thetis that the bravest man before Ilium shall have her slain son's arms. Agamemnon must make the fateful decision, and it is Odysseus and not Ajax who receives the gift of Hephæstus-forged armor. Ajax is lashed by human anger and a craving for vengeance in a proportion to match his heroic capacities. But before these impulses can be expressed, there is an intervention by Athene: Ajax is struck mad and slaughters the captive Trojan livestock, cursing Agamemnon, Odysseus, and Menelaus the while, in a manner that would be described today as a massive displacement of aggression. It is Athene, then, who saves Ajax from a more direct expression of his fury and saves the Greeks from a slaughter of their leaders. Again the ingenious and rational intervention of the gods, a formal working out of internal plight in a tightly woven and dramatic plot. It is much as Professor Dodds has suggested in examining the containment of irrationality in Greek myth. The clouding and bewildering of judgment that is *ate,* or the seemingly unnatural access of courage that is *menos*—both of these sources of potential disruption of natural order are attributed to an external agency, to a supernatural intervention, whether of the gods or of the Erinyes.

I suggest that in general the inward monition, or the sudden unaccountable feeling of power, or the sudden unaccountable loss of judgment, is the germ out of which the divine machinery developed. One result of transposing the event from the interior to the external world is that the vagueness is eliminated: the indeterminate daemon has to be made concrete as some particular personal god.[1]

These were the gods that the Greeks shared, by virtue of whom a sense of causation became communal, through the nurturing of whom an art form emerged. The alternative, as Philip Rahv comments in discussing the governess in *The Turn of the Screw* and the chief protagonist in *The Beast in the Jungle,* is to give up one's allotment of experience. If one cannot externalize the daemon where it can be enmeshed in the texture of aesthetic experience, then the last resort is to freeze and block: the over-repression and denial treated so perceptively by Freud in *The Problem of Anxiety.*

What is the art form of the myth? Principally it is drama, yet for all its concern with preternatural forces and characters, it is realistic drama that in the phrase of Wellek and Warren tells of "origins and destinies." As they put it, it comprises "the explanations a society offers its young of why the world is and why we do as we do, its pedagogic images of the nature and destiny of man." [2] Ernst Cassirer senses a proper antinomy when he notes that the myth somehow emphasizes the physiognomic character of experience while at the same time it has the property of compelling belief. Its power is that it lives on the feather line between fantasy and reality. It must be neither too good nor too bad to be true, nor must it be too true. And if it is the case that art as a mode of knowing has precisely the function of connecting through metaphor what before had no apparent kinship, then in the present case the art form of the myth connects the daemonic world of impulse with the world of reason by a verisimilitude that conforms to each.

But there is a paradox. For on the one side we speak of myth as an externalization, on the other we speak of it as a pedagogical image. This is surely a strange source of instruction! But it is precisely here that the dramatic form of the myth becomes significant, precisely here where Gilbert Murray was so perceptive of the genius of Homer and of the Greeks: "This power of entering vividly into the feelings of both parties in a conflict is . . . the characteristic gift." [3]

Let me revert for a moment to a consideration of the human personality, to the nature of the vicissitudes that are externalized in myth. It is no longer novel to speak of personality as a cast of characters, although in the last decades we have oversimplified the drama they enact in the summary image of Freud's morality play of the ego, superego, and id. In his telling essay on "The Poet and the Daydream," Freud recognizes the potential complexity of the internal cast when he speaks of the art of the playwright as one of decomposing this cast into the dramatis personae of the staged drama. It is far from clear why our discordant impulses are bound and structured in a set of identities—why one pattern of impulse is the self-pitying little man in us, another the nurturing protector, another the voice of moral indignation. Surely it is something more than the sum of identifications we have undertaken in the course of achieving balances between love and independence, coming to terms with those who have touched our lives. Here myth becomes the tutor, the shaper of identities; it is here that personality imitates myth in as deep a sense as myth is an externalization of the vicissitudes of personality.

Joseph Campbell, in his *The Hero with a Thousand Faces,* writes: [4]

> In his life-form the individual is necessarily only a fraction and distortion of the total image of man. He is limited either as male or as female; at any given period of his life he is again limited as child, youth, mature adult, or ancient; furthermore, in his life role he is necessarily specialized as craftsman, tradesman, servant, or thief, priest, leader, wife, nun, or harlot; he cannot be all. Hence the totality—the fullness of man—is not in the separate member, but in the body of the society as a whole; the individual can be only an organ.

But if no man is all, there is at least in what Campbell calls the "mythologically instructed community" a corpus of images and identities and models that provides the pattern to which growth may aspire—a range of metaphoric identities. We are accustomed to speaking of myth in this programmatic sense in reference to history, as when Sorel invokes the general strike of all workers as a dynamizing image, or when

Christians speak of the Second Coming for which men must prepare themselves. In the same sense one may speak of the corpus of myth as providing a set of possible programmatic identities for the individual personality. It would perhaps be more appropriate to say that the mythologically instructed community provides its members with a library of scripts upon which the individual may judge the internal drama of his multiple identities. For myth, as I shall now try to illustrate, serves not only as a pattern to which one aspires, but also as a criterion for the self-critic.

Let me use as an example the myths that embody and personify man's capacity for happiness. They are not infinite in variety, but varied enough. An early version is the Greek conception of the Five Ages of Man, the first of which is the happy Age of Gold. In Robert Graves's transliteration: [5] "These men were the so-called golden race, subjects of Cronus, who lived without cares or labor, eating only acorns, wild fruit, and honey that dripped from the trees . . . never growing old, dancing, and laughing much; death to them was no more terrible than sleep. They are all gone now, but their spirits survive as happy genii." This is the myth of happiness as innocence, and in the Christian tradition we know it as Man before the Fall. Innocence ends either by a successful attempt to steal the knowledge of God or by aspiring to the cognitive power of the gods, *hubris*. And with the end of innocence, there is an end to happiness. Knowledge is equated with temptation to evil. The issue appears to revolve around the acquisition and uses of knowledge.

Let me oversimplify in the interest of brevity and say that from these early myths there emerge two types of mythic plot: the plot of innocence and the plot of cleverness—the former being a kind of Arcadian ideal, requiring the eschewal of complexity and awareness, the latter requiring the cultivation of competence almost to the point of guile. The happy childhood, the good man as the child of God, the simple plowman, the Rousseauian ideal of natural nobility—these are the creatures of the plot of innocence. At the other extreme there are Penelope, the suitors, and Odysseus. In Gilbert Murray's words: [6]

Penelope—she has just learned on good evidence that Odysseus is alive and will return immediately—suddenly determines that she cannot put off the suitors any longer, but brings down her husband's bow, and says she will forthwith marry the man who can shoot through twelve axeheads with it! Odysseus hears her and is pleased! May it not be that in the original story there was a reason for Penelope to bring the bow, and for Odysseus to be pleased? It was a plot. He [Odysseus] meant Eurycleia [the old maidservant] to recognize him [by his scar], to send the maids away, and break the news to Penelope. Then husband and wife together arranged the trial of the bow.

Again and again in the Greek myths there are cleverness, competence and artifice—Herakles, Achilles, Odysseus, Perseus—wherever you may look. It is the happy triumph of clever competence with a supernatural assist. And yet there is also the ideal of the Age of Innocence. So too in the later Christian tradition and in our own times. The manner in which superior knowledge shows itself changes: the ideal of the crafty warrior, the wise man, the interpreter of the word of God, the Renaissance omnicompetent, the wily merchant, the financial wizard, the political genius. If it is true that in some way each is suspect, it is also true that each is idealized in his own way. Each is presented as satisfied. New versions arise to reflect the ritual and practice of each era—the modifications of the happiness of innocence and the satisfaction of competence.

I would like to submit that the manner in which man has striven for competence and longed for innocence has reflected the controlling myths of the community. The medieval scholar, the Florentine prince, the guild craftsman alike, as well as the withdrawn monastic of Thomas à Kempis and the mendicant of St. Francis—all of these are deeply involved with the myths of innocence and competence, and are formed by them. Indeed, the uncertainty in resolving the dichotomy of reason and revelation as ways to a knowledge of God reflects the duality of the myth of happiness and salvation. It is not simply society that patterns itself on the idealizing myths, but unconsciously it is the individual man as well who is able to structure his internal clamor of identities in terms of prevailing myth. Life then produces myth and finally imitates it.

In our own time, in the American culture, there is a deep problem generated by the confusion that has befallen the myth of the happy man. It reflects itself in the American personality. There still lingers the innocent Christian conception that happiness is the natural state of man—or at least of the child and of man as innocent—and that it is something that we have done or failed to do as individuals that creates a rather Protestantized and private unhappiness. The impact of Freud has begun to destroy this myth, to replace it. Our popular films may now, with artistry, depict the child as murderer. A generation of playwrights have destroyed the remnant of Horatio Alger, replacing it with the image of Arthur Miller's salesman dying by entropy, an object of compassion. We are no longer, in Professor Campbell's words, "a mythologically instructed community." And so one finds a new generation struggling to find or to create a satisfactory and challenging mythic image as aspiration.

Two such images seem to be emerging in the new generation. One is the myth of the "hipsters" and the "squares." The other is the myth of creative wholeness. The first is the myth of the wandering hero as uncommitted, as capable of the hour's subjectivity—its "kicks"—sharing in a new inwardness. It is the theme of reduction to the essentially personal, the hero capable of filtering out the clamors of an outside world, an almost masturbatory ideal. Eugene Burdick in a recent issue of *The Reporter* (3 April 1958) gives the following account of a conversation in a San Francisco café between two practitioners of the cult of the Beat Generation:

"Man, I remember something when I was little, a boy," somebody named Lee says. He is hunched forward, his elbows on the table, a tumbler of wine between his hands. "About a dog. Little miserable dog of mine."

"Yeah, man, go on," Mike says, his eyes lighting up.

"I get up real early to do my paper route. Los Angeles *Examiner*," Lee says. "Streets always empty, just a few milk trucks and bakery trucks and other kids like me. My dog goes along, see? Every day he trots along with me. Little mongrel dog."

"Yeah, yeah, go on, man," Mike says, impatient for the story, sure that it has meaning.

"There we are in all those big empty streets. Just me and the dog. Sun coming up, papers falling on the porches, me dreaming and walking and the dog trotting," Lee says. "Then far away, about as big as a black mosquito, I see this hopped-up Model A. Wonderful pipes on it, blatting so sweet I could hear them for six blocks. I stand there on the curb, listening to that sweet sound and watching that car come weaving down that empty street. And the dog stands in the gutter, watching too. That Model A gets bigger and I can see the chrome pipes on the side, the twin Strombergs sucking air, just eating up the asphalt."

He pauses and Mike leans forward and says urgently, "Now, man, come on, go. I wanna hear this."

"This Model A is a roadster and there is a Mexican driving and his girl with him," Lee says slowly, stalking the climax. "It weaves across the street, and me and the dog stare at it. And it comes for us in a big slow curve and hit that dog. His back broke in mid-air and he was dead when he hit the street again. Like a big man cracking a seed in his teeth . . . same sound, I mean. And the girl stares back at me and laughs. And I laugh. You see why, man?"

The two of them sit quietly, looking down at the wine and listening to the jazz. Mike glances once at Lee and then back at his glass. He has learned something secret and private about Lee, and that is good enough. After a while they sit back, smiling, and listen to the jazz.

It is not easy to create a myth and to emulate it at the same time. James Dean and Kerouac, Kingsley Amis and John Osborne, the Teddy Boys and the hipsters: they do not make a mythological community. They represent mythmaking in process as surely as Hemingway's characters did in their time, Scott Fitzgerald's in theirs. What is ultimately clear is that even the attempted myth must be a model for imitating, a programmatic drama to be tried on for fit. One sees the identities of a group of young men being "packaged" in terms of the unbaked myth. It is a mold, a prescription of characters, a plot. Whether the myth will be viable, whether it will fit the internal plight, we do not know. There are temporary myths too. There was a myth of the supernatural birth of a dead woman's son, a myth Boas found in 1888 and again in 1900. By 1931 there was no trace of it.

What of the renewal of the myth of the full, creative man? It is even more inchoate than the first, yet perhaps more important. It is, for example, the young middle-aged executive

sent back to the university by the company for a year, want-
ing humanities and not sales engineering; it is this man telling you that he would rather take life classes Saturday
morning at the Museum School than be president of the
company; it is the adjectival extravaganza of the word "creative," as in creative advertising, creative engineering, creative
writing. It is as if, given the demise of the myths of creation
and their replacement by a scientific cosmogony that for all
its formal beauty lacks metaphoric force, the theme of creating becomes internalized, creating anguish rather than, as
in the externalized myths, providing a basis for psychic relief
and sharing. Yet, this self-contained image of creativity becomes, I think, the basis for a myth of happiness. But perhaps
between the death of one myth and the birth of its replacement there must be a reinternalization, even to the point of
a *culte de moi*. That we cannot yet know. All that is certain
is that we live in a period of mythic confusion that may provide the occasion for a new growth of myth, myth more suitable for our times.

Indeed, one may ask whether the rise of the novel as an art
form, and particularly the subjectification of the novel since
the middle of the nineteenth century, whether these do not
symbolize the voyage into the interior that comes with the
failure of prevailing myths to provide external models toward which one may aspire. For when the prevailing myths
fail to fit the varieties of man's plight, frustration expresses
itself first in mythoclasm and then in the lonely search for
internal identity. The novels of Conrad, of Hardy, of Gide,
of Camus—paradoxically enough, they provide man with
guides for the internal search. One of Graham Greene's most
tormented books, an autobiographical fragment on an African voyage, is entitled *Journey Without Maps*. Perhaps the
modern novel, in contrast to the myth, is the response to
the internal anguish that can find no external constraint in
the form of myth, a form of internal map. But this is a matter
requiring a closer scrutiny than we can give it here. Suffice it
to say that the alternative to externalization in myth appears
to be the internalization of the personal novel, the first a
communal effort, the second the lone search for identity.

Let me conclude by reiterating the general line of my

thesis. It is simple enough. The first premise is that the externalization of inner impulse in the form of myth provides the basis for a sharing of inner experience and makes possible the work of art that has as its objective to contain and cleanse the terror from impulse. The myth as a work of art has as its principal form the shape of drama. So too the human personality: its patternings of impulse express themselves as identities in an internal drama. The myths that are the treasure of an instructed community provide the models and the programs in terms of which the growth of the internal cast of identities is molded and enspirited. And finally, when the myths no longer fit the internal plights of those who require them, the transition to newly created myths may take the form of a chaotic voyage into the interior, the certitudes of externalization replaced by the anguish of the internal voyage.

NOTES

1 E. R. Dodds, *The Greeks and the Irrational* (Boston: The Beacon Press, 1957), pp. 14-15.

2 René Wellek and Austin Warren, *Theory of Literature* (New York: Harcourt, Brace & Co., 1942), p. 180.

3 Gilbert Murray, *The Literature of Ancient Greece* (Chicago: University of Chicago Press, Phoenix edition, 1957), p. 43.

4 Joseph Campbell, *The Hero with a Thousand Faces* (New York: Meridian Books, Inc., 1956), pp. 382-383.

5 Reprinted from *The Greek Myths*, by Robert Graves. Published by Penguin Books Inc., 3300 Clipper Mill Road, Baltimore 11, Maryland.

6 Murray, *op. cit.*, pp. 39-40.

SUGGESTIONS FOR DISCUSSION

1. According to Bruner's account, what relationship does a participant in myth (hearer, teller, reader) have to the myth itself? Which of Murray's "effects" of myth concern Bruner?

2. How is it, according to Bruner, that externalization of human anxieties and impulses can produce myths that are suitable models for conduct?

3. Bruner claims that externalization, in conscious literature at any rate, is no longer producing adequate mythic images. If not, might the failure be related to the kind of psychic element which contemporary artists choose to externalize? And does that choice seem related to present conditions?

4. Why are men like Mike and Lee not strong candidates for mythic herohood?

5. What counts against the "internal voyage" as a subject for myth?
6. How does externalization, as Bruner describes it, differ from the poetic and mythic process described by Frye? How might the two theories be combined into a more general theory of poetic or mythic creation?

A MYTH FOR THE FUTURE?*

HENRY A. MURRAY

Among the interrelated instigating situations which distress the world today, more particularly the Western world and Western individuals as persons, the following are perceived by many people: (a) the probability of the mutual extermination of the technologically more advanced nations of the two Northern Hemispheres; (b) the aggressive, world-ambitious mystique (apocalyptic ideology) of Communism in the East and the absence of any comparably dynamic, world-unifying vision in the West; (c) the hypertrophy of greed for material possessions and comforts, and for individual and national power and prestige based on such possessions, constituting, on the one hand, the principal, irresistible forces productive of fierce, global competitions for markets and resources, and eventually of a genocidal war; and on the other hand, within each nation, resulting in a gigantic, heart-breaking disproportion of matter, mechanisms, and shallow, regulated social contacts *over* spirit, depth of thought and feeling, joyous spontaneities, and quality of interpersonal relations; (d) the senescence of the traditional religions and their present incapacity in the face of the world's strait to bring forth

---

* These suggestive paragraphs originally formed the conclusion of the long article which is partly reprinted in the beginning of this volume under the title "Definitions of Myth." Murray's title for this short section was "Challenge."

a new vision of a better world, to generate widespread passionate belief in their own doctrines, or, in all sincerity, to
guide individual self-development and conduct in the light
of an acceptable ideal, and *partly* because of the unfilled
vacuum left by the decay of these religions, the spread of
existential anxiety, affectlessness, meaninglessness, spiritual
loneliness, hollowness, alienation, and regressive emotional
drift (the "Beat" phenomenon).

Instigations of these vast dimensions are too appalling to be
held steadily in mind by more than a few people. The majority, made anxious by such prospects, repress them and go
about their own affairs. But this being one of the most
momentous instances in human history of Challenge, as
Toynbee would say, there must be some potential, creative
Response latent in the unconscious depths of a good many
Western people. I have already discussed several channels of
response—covert mythic visions, theoretical and ideological
constructions, experimental actions and directions of individual development, and, in conjunction with these, mythic
works of art. But, so far as I can see, there are no known
mythic patterns which are appropriate to the magnitude and
exigency of the confronting situation. To succeed, I would
surmise, they will have to be as radical and revolutionary as
the antibiological Sermon on the Mount.

Would it be less revolutionary or more revolutionary, from
the point of view of our innate store of self-serving, egocen-
tric instincts, to suggest that the mystique of the hero, savior,
charismatic leader, or great man—Christ or Caesar—and the
mystique of the elect minority with a mission, of inflated
nationalism, or the great nation are all obsolete? If so, what
would our instincts say to a procession of myths in which
there were never less than two chief characters—two leaders
meeting amicably at the summit, two nations settling their
disputes, rituals cementing international reciprocities and
concord; and, on the personal level also, never less than two
chief characters, man and woman, in a creative, mutually
self-developing relationship?

SUGGESTIONS FOR DISCUSSION

1. Do beginnings exist in America today of the sort of myth Murray looks for?
2. What signs are there in advertising, television, the slick magazines, and so on, of an incipient myth of material possessions? How do you think Murray would look on such a myth, judging from what he asks of myths in general? Bruner?

BIBLIOGRAPHY

MYTHS, LEGENDS, ETC.

When many English editions of a work exist, no particular translation or edition is listed.

Apuleius, *The Golden Ass.*

Arnason, Jón, *Icelandic Legends,* tr. George E. J. Powell and Eríkr Magnússon (London, 1864-1866). 2 vols.

Banks, Theodore Howard Jr., tr., *Sir Gawain and the Green Knight* (New York, 1929).

Bellows, Henry Adams, tr., *Edda Saemundar, The Poetic Edda* (New York, 1923). 2 vols.

Benedict, Ruth, *Zuni Mythology* (New York, 1935).

Blake, William, *The Marriage of Heaven and Hell.*

Boas, Franz, *Kwakiutl Tales* (New York, 1910). 2 vols.

Boccaccio, Giovanni, *The Decameron.*

Bullfinch, Thomas, *The Age of Fable* (Boston, 1894).

Burton, Richard F., tr., *Arabian Nights* (Bombay, 1885). 10 vols.

Calloway, Henry, *Nursery Tales and Traditions of the Zulus* (London, 1868).

Campbell, J. F., *Popular Tales of the West Highlands* (London, 1890). 4 vols.

Campbell, Joseph, ed., *The Portable Arabian Nights* (New York, 1952).

Cendrars, Blaise, *The African Saga* (New York, 1927).

Chaucer, Geoffrey, *The Canterbury Tales.*

Colum, Padraic, *A Treasury of Irish Folklore* (New York, 1954).

Crane, Thomas Frederick, *Italian Popular Tales* (Boston, 1885).

Curtin, Jeremiah, *Myths and Folk-Lore of Ireland* (Boston, 1890).

——, *Seneca Indian Myths* (New York, 1923).

Dante, *The Divine Comedy.*

Dasent, G. W., *East O' the Sun and West O' the Moon* (New York, 1917).

Davids, Mrs. Rhys, *Stories of the Buddha* (London and New York, no date).

Davis, F. Hadland, *Myths & Legends of Japan* (New York, no date).

Eberhard, Wolfram, *Chinese Fairy Tales and Folk Tales* (London, 1937).

Elwin, Verrier, *Myths of Middle India* (Oxford, 1949).

Faulkner, William, *The Bear*.

Frobenius, Leo, and Douglas C. Fox, *African Genesis* (New York, 1927).

Gade, Helen and John, tr., *Norwegian Fairy Tales from the Collection of Asbjörnsen and Moe* (New York, 1924).

Ginzberg, Louis, *The Legends of the Jews* (Philadelphia, 1911). 7 vols.

Glover, W. J., ed., *British Fairy and Folk Tales* (London, 1920).

Goodwin, Grenville, *Myths and Tales of the White Mountain Apache*, Memoirs of the American Folk-Lore Society, Vol. XXXIII (New York, 1939).

Gray, Louis Herbert, *The Mythology of All Races* (Boston, 1916-1931). 13 vols. (Includes surveys of Greek, Roman, Teutonic, Celtic, Slavic, Finno-Ugric, Siberian, Semitic, Indian, Iranian, Armenian, African, Chinese, Japanese, Oceanic, North American, Central American, Egyptian and Far Eastern mythology.)

Grey, Sir George, *Polynesian Mythology, and Ancient Traditional History of the New Zealand Race, as Furnished by their Priests and Chiefs* (London, 1855).

Grimm, Jacob and Wilhelm, *Fairy Tales*.

Guest, Lady Charlotte E., tr., *The Mabinogion,* Everyman's Library (London, 1906).

Hapgood, Isabel Florence, *The Epic Songs of Russia* (New York, 1886).

Harris, Joel Chandler, *Uncle Remus, His Songs and His Sayings* (New York, 1881).

The Holy Bible.

Homer, *The Odyssey, The Iliad.*

Hull, Eleanor, *The Cuchullin Saga in Irish Literature* (London, 1898).

Hume, Robert Ernest, *The Thirteen Principal Upanishads, Translated from the Sanskrit* (Oxford, 1931).

In-Sŏb, Zong, *Folk Tales from Korea* (London, 1952).

Jacobus de Varagine, *The Golden Legend,* tr. Granger Ryan and Helmut Ripperger (London, 1941). 2 vols.

Jones, Gwyn, *Welsh Legends and Folk-Tales* (Oxford, 1955).

Kennedy, Charles W., tr., *Beowulf* (New York, 1940).

King, L. W., *Babylonian Religion and Mythology* (New York, 1899).

Kirby, William Forsell, tr., *Kalevala, The Land of Heroes,* Everyman's Library (London, 1907).

Kramer, S. N., *Sumerian Mythology,* American Philosophical Society Memoirs, Vol. XXI (Philadelphia, 1944).

Lawrence, D. H., *The Man Who Died.*

Loomis, Roger Sherman, tr., *The Romance of Tristram and Ysolt, by Thomas of Britain* (New York, 1931).

Lorimer, D. L. R. and E. O., *Persian Tales* (London, 1914).

Magnus, Leonard A., *Russian Folk-Tales* (London, 1915).

Malory, Thomas, *Le Morte d'Arthur*, ed. Ernest Rhys, Everyman's Library (New York, 1906). 2 vols.

Milton, John, *Paradise Lost.*

Morris, William, *Sigurd the Volsung.*

Nivedita, Sister, and Ananda K. Coomaraswamy, *Myths of the Hindus and Buddhists* (New York, 1914).

Opler, Morris Edward, *Myths and Legends of the Lipan Apache Indians,* Memoirs of the American Folk-Lore Society, Vol. XXXVI (New York, 1940).

Orwell, George, *1984.*

Ovid, *Metamorphoses.*

Sherwood, Merriam, tr., *The Song of Roland* (New York, 1938).

Smith, W. Ramsay, *Myths and Legends of the Australian Aboriginals* (London, 1930).

Snorri Sturluson, *Edda Snorru Sturlusonor,* tr. Arthur Gilchrist (New York, 1916).

Stimson, J. F., *The Legends of Maui and Tahaki,* Bernice P. Bishop Museum Bulletin, No. 127 (Honolulu, 1934).

Tatlock, Jessie M., *Greek and Roman Mythology* (New York, 1917).

Thompson, Stith, *Tales of the North American Indians* (Cambridge, Mass., 1929).

Thorpe, Benjamin, *Northern Mythology* (London, 1851-1852). 3 vols.

Von Schiefner, F. Anton, and W. R. S. Ralston, *Tibetan Tales, Derived from Indian Sources* (London, 1906).

Warren, Henry Clarke, *Buddhism in Translation,* Harvard Oriental Series, 3 (Cambridge, Mass., 1896).

Way, Arthur S., tr., *The Lay of the Nibelung Men* (Cambridge, England, 1911).

Werner, Alice, *Myths & Legends of the Bantu* (London, 1933).

Werner, E. T. C., *Myths & Legends of China* (London, 1922).

Williams, Alfred, *Tales from the Panchatantra* (Oxford, 1930).

Wood, Clement, *Dreams: Their Meaning and Practical Application* (New York, 1931).

Wratislaw, A. H. *Sixty Folk-Tales from Exclusively Slavic Sources* (London, 1899).

Yeats, William Butler, *The Collected Poems of W. B. Yeats* (New York, 1952).

——, *Irish Fairy and Folk Tales,* Modern Library (New York, no date).

Zeydel, Edwin H., and Bayard Quincy Morgan, *The Parzival of Wolfram von Eschenbach* (Chapel Hill, 1951).

TOPICS FOR RESEARCH

Each of the following topics presupposes familiarity with one of the myths, tales, or collections of myths and tales listed in the Bibliography.

1. To what extent does the myth you have chosen satisfy Murray's definitions?
2. What evidence do you find in it of the psychic processes outlined by Bruner? By Frye?
3. What kind of interpretation seems appropriate to the myth—the sort recommended by Dorson? The sort practiced by Eliade? By Campbell? No interpretation at all?
4. Analyze the myth in terms of the themes it contains, in the manner of Kluckhohn or Campbell.
5. Analyze the myth in terms of its possible causes and functions (see Murray).
6. What signs are there that the myth may have acted as a model or standard for human conduct? What human qualities does it extol or condemn? Could it serve as a model today?
7. Consider the question of *validity:* For whom, and in what sense, might the myth be thought of as false? As true?
8. Is there potential meaning in the myth for contemporary Americans? What modifications in its content and theme would seem necessary in order for it to appeal to Americans?
9. Is there potential in the myth for influence on historical events and national ideologies, as with the myth of the three Romes?
10. Does the myth build on or imply a "topocosm," in Frye's sense of the word?